Abbreviation

The following books and essays written by Jameson are indicated by initials:

AF   *Archaeologies of the Future: The Desire Called Utopia and Other Science Fictions*

BM   *Brecht and Method*

CM   'Cognitive Mapping'

CT   *The Cultural Turn: Selected Writings on the Postmodern, 1983–1998*

DD   '*Dekalog* as *Decameron*'

ET   'The End of Temporality'

F1   'Foreword', in Algirdas Julien Greimas, *On Meaning: Selected Writings in Semiotics Theory*

F2   'Foreword', in Jean- François Lyotard, *The Postmodern Condition: A Report on Knowledge*

FA   *Fables of Aggression: Wyndham Lewis, the Modernist as Fascist*

FC   'Future City'

FLH   'Flaubert's Libidinal Historicism: *Trois Contes*'

FMA   'From Metaphor to Allegory'

GAH   'The Great American Hunter: Ideological Content in the Novel'

IFJ   'Interview with Fredric Jameson'

IT1   *The Ideologies of Theory: Essays 1971–1986.* Volume 1: *Situations of Theory*

IT2   *The Ideologies of Theory: Essays 1971–1986.* Volume 2: *Syntax of History*

LM   *Late Marxism: Adorno, or, The Persistence of the Dialectic*

MA   'Marc Angenot, Literary History, and the Study of Culture in the Nineteenth Century'

MF   *Marxism and Form: Twentieth-Century Dialectical Theories of Literature*

MI   'Modernism and Imperialism'

MPL	'Marx's Purloined Letter'
OCS	'On Cultural Studies'
PCL	*Postmodernism, or, the Cultural Logic of Late Capitalism*
PD	'Persistencies of the Dialectic: Three Sites'
PH	*The Prison-House of Language: A Critical Account of Structuralism and Russian Formalism*
PU	*The Political Unconscious: Narrative as a Socially Symbolic Act*
RG	'On Representing Globalisation'
RP	'Regarding Postmodernism: A Conversation with Fredric Jameson'
RS	'Rimbaud and the Spatial Text'
S	*Sartre: The Origins of a Style*
SM	*A Singular Modernity: Essay on the Ontology of the Present*
ST	*The Seeds of Time*
STS	'Symptoms of Theory or Symptoms for Theory?'
SV	*Signatures of the Visible*
TL	'Towards a Libidinal Economy of Three Modern Painters'
U	'"Ulysses" in History'
WS	'Wallace Stevens'

The following texts by other authors are also indicated by initials.

OP	P. Anderson, *The Origins of Postmodernity*
SO	S. Žižek, *The Sublime Object of Ideology*
TN	S. Žižek, *Tarrying with the Negative: Kant, Hegel, and the Critique of Ideology*

Fredric Jameson: Live Theory

Also available from the series:

Fredric Jameson: Live Theory

Ian Buchanan

continuum

Continuum International Publishing Group
The Tower Building   80 Maiden Lane
11 York Road   Suite 704
London SE1 7NX   New York
                            NY 10038

British Library Cataloguing-in-Publication Data
A catalogue record for this book is available from the British Library.

ISBN: 0–8264–9108–1 (hardback)   0–8264–9109–X (paperback)

Library of Congress Cataloging-in-Publication Data
A catalog record for this book is available from the Library of Congress.

Typeset by RefineCatch Limited, Bungay, Suffolk
Printed and bound in Great Britain by
MPG Books Ltd, Bodmin, Cornwall

For Fredric Jameson

Contents

Acknowledgements

I would like to thank Fredric Jameson for all his assistance over the years in making available both his time and his archive and for suffering the importunate questions of a student who never had the courtesy to enrol in his courses. His is an example of scholarship, political commitment and comradeship one can but aspire to. I must give special thanks to Darren Jorgensen for his invaluable research assistance and incisive commentary on various drafts. I must also thank Roland Boer, Maria Elisa Cevasco, Wang Fengzhen, Peter Fitting, Sean Homer, Caren Irr, Noel King, Andrew Milner, Alberto Moreiras, Negar Mottahedeh, David Savat, Imre Szeman, as well as the many other 'Fred-heads' it has been my good fortune to meet and share a beer with – each, in their own way, stimulated me to see Jameson's work differently, as always richer than I had hitherto noticed.

Lastly I must thank Tanya Buchanan . . . *we are still going you and I.*

Cardiff, May 2006

Chapter 1

Dialectical Criticism

> The works of culture come to us as signs in an all-but-forgotten code, as symptoms of diseases no longer even recognised as such, as fragments of a totality we have long since lost the organs to see.
>
> Fredric Jameson, *Marxism and Form*

It seems unnecessary to argue for the significance of Fredric Jameson. Jameson's work has done more to shape our consciousness of ourselves as an emergent global society than any other thinker. So following the path blazed by his own book on Brecht, I intend to argue for the usefulness of Jameson. My central exhibit will be his method of critical analysis called 'dialectical criticism'. Handled properly dialectical criticism should shock us, Jameson insists, with the same 'sickening shudder we feel in an elevator's fall or in the sudden dip in an airliner' (*MF*, 308), because this viscerally reminds us of our role as participant observers in the world-historical situation we call everyday life. Shock is basic to and indeed 'constitutive of the dialectic as such: without this transformational moment, without this initial conscious transcendence of an older, more naïve position, there can be no question of any genuinely dialectical coming to consciousness' (*MF*, 308). No reader of Jameson can have failed to have had this heady experience at least once – it is his consistent ability to transform our understanding of the cultural sphere that makes him one of the most important cultural critics of the twentieth century.

So basic is this shock to the function and purpose of dialectical criticism, its absence can be read as the sure sign that our approach is not yet broken free of the shackles of habit and tradition and passed through the gates of the dialectic. This in turn tells us something about the twofold aim and purpose of dialectical criticism, which is to demystify the present, on the one hand, by revealing the ways in which a particular state of affairs is secretly organized so as to advantage one class fraction or another in a particular local struggle, and on the other hand to open up a space for thoughts of the future (*MF*, 381). The implication here, which underpins all of Jameson's work, is that class interest (in this precise, relational and indeed conflictual sense) cannot be given direct expression – it is the *ultimate* obscenity, and it is the job of dialectical criticism to uncover the various means culture has of censoring and disguising it, but nonetheless in the manner of all obscene thoughts communicating it all the same. 'It is an often-taught and often-forgotten lesson that ideology is designed to promote the human dignity and clear conscience of a given class at the same time that it discredits their adversaries' (*MF*, 380). Class conflict is, then, the ultimate reality it is the task of dialectical criticism to reconstruct. It is this knowledge, which can only be won via the patient and comprehensive reconstruction of the historical situation of a text, that produces the constitutive shock of dialectical criticism. Historical reconstruction, which is to say interpretation, should not be conceived as the movement from one specialized area of discourse – literature – to another – history or economics – but from the abstract to the concrete (*MF*, 377). If an image of this mode of thought is needed, then it should be envisaged as the multiplication of horizons in which the text is maintained and the multiplication of perspectives from which it is seen (*MF*, 390).[1]

'I have found it useful' Jameson writes in a late and extremely valuable *aperçu* on the fate of the dialectic in contemporary theory, 'to characterise the dialectic in three different ways, which surely do not exhaust the possibilities, but may at least clarify the discussion and also alert us to possible confusions or category mistakes, to interferences between them' (*PD*, 360). The three ways of characterizing the dialectic are: (1) in terms of reflexivity, as a necessary second-guessing or reconsideration of the very terms and concepts of one's analytic apparatus; (2) in terms of a problematization of causality and historical narrative; and (3) in terms of the production of contradiction. The third form is the most developed in Jameson's work and finds its most refined expression in his account of what he calls 'metacommentary', which is as near as he comes to offering a 'method' (but as will be seen, it is a method that needs to be adapted and altered according to the demands of the specific case at hand). Needless to say, these three ways of conceiving the dialectic should not be seen as in any way mutually exclusive of one another. It would be much more accurate to see them as the three sides of triangle.

Reflexivity

The basic story dialectical criticism has to tell is one of reversal, 'that paradoxical turning around of a phenomenon into its opposite of which the transformation of quantity into quality is only one of the better known manifestations. It can be described as a kind of leap-frogging affair in time, in which the drawbacks of a given historical situation turn out in reality to be its secret advantages, in which what looked like built-in superiorities suddenly prove to be the most ironclad limits on its future developments' (*MF*, 309). Peter Wollen's marvellous short history of the development of cinema, written from the perspective of technical innovations in film stock, offers a vivid, if benign (Jameson's own rather pointed choice of illustration is the history of the development of nuclear missiles) illustration of this.[2] Just at the moment when black and white film had achieved a sufficient standard of technical sophistication to enable filming to be done on location more at less at will, essentially liberating both the camera and the narrative from the closeting confines of the studio, colour film was introduced. As transformative of the look of film colour would prove to be, its lighting requirements were such that in the early years, at least, location shooting was almost impossible.

So even as film began to look more realistic than it had ever been able to before when shot exclusively in black and white, the constraints of the studio gave the stories a feeling of artificiality quite at odds with the look. No sooner had audiences gotten used to expansive stories in which the camera ranged far and wide, they were thrust back inside the claustrophobic box of drawing-room dramas. But once colour was introduced, black and white films immediately began to seem less expressive than they used to, their 'reality effect' loss its efficacy, until at a supreme moment of reversal black and white became (as it is now) the 'sign' of art-house expressionism. In deciding whether to shoot in black and white or colour, directors had to choose between looking real, but feeling artificial and feeling real, but looking artificial. Consequently, certain types of films were simply impossible to make, while others instantly appeared more attractive than hitherto: in effect, the western was stopped dead in its tracks at the high point of its generic development, while the costume drama and the musical knew a sudden and dramatic change of fortune. The disadvantage of the artificiality of colour and the confinement to the studio was turned into an advantage by the fantasy setting of the musical which foregrounded spectacle and intense movement not verisimilitude.[3]

But to be able to tell this particular story of reversal, of the advantages and disadvantages of one film stock versus another, film stock itself has to be isolated as an appropriate factor around which to base a history of cinema. This moment – that of the initial choice of historical variables around which to construct the story – is, then, the first and doubtless most consequential moment of dialectical criticism (*MF*, 311). The question that has to be confronted now – namely, how does one decide which variables are appropriate for staging a particular type of history – is of both methodological and epistemological concern. Getting the choice wrong will obviously prove disastrous, but to say this already assumes it is always possible to make a choice in the first place and that is by no means certain. Faced with so complex a story as the development of an entire artistic medium, particularly one whose take-off was as rapid and widespread as cinema's was, how would one settle on any single factor as being decisive? Are there not any number of rival choices that, comparatively speaking, might not have served just as well? There is no definitive answer to this question, but Jameson does provide some guidelines which can assist us in deciding whether our choices are legitimate or not.

To begin with, it must be relational, as our example above clearly is in the way it calls attention to the technological factors impacting on the artistic choices to do with setting and narrative, thereby raising questions about those choices we might not have otherwise considered. We have to take care, however, that our choice of starting point is genuinely transhistorical, otherwise we wind up drawing our own eye (to use Jameson's marvellous phrase): for instance, the literary device of 'point of view' reflects the historical situation of the middle class at the time of its invention in the mid-eighteenth century, therefore it is inappropriate, Jameson argues, to use it as an anchor point for a literary history spanning, say, from mediaeval times to our own, and encompassing a range of literary materials, such as folk songs and so forth, besides the novel (*MF*, 358). It gives us a false view of the past as an underdeveloped foretaste of the present and makes all other forms of literary production seem like unconscious precursors of the novel, when in fact present patterns of literary production would not have been suited to periods before their own. Isolating a particular stylistic effect or technique in this way produces not a transhistorical category, capable of cracking open the opacities of the past, but rather its opposite, an ahistorical category which turns the past into a photonegative of the present.[4]

What is missing from our truncated history of the development of cinema is any consideration of audience sensibilities, that is to say, factors above and beyond the immediate determinations of technological innovation. However convenient it may have been for studios to concentrate their productions in the area of musicals, given the technological constraints imposed by the introduction of colour film, this would have been a commercial disaster if audiences had not kept pace. 'So it is that the vexed question of historical determinism slowly comes into view before us, even in what seemed to be a purely literary context' (*MF*, 359). For while we may plausibly say that technological change forced cinema to adapt to the new range of possibilities colour made available, we cannot say that technological change alone forced audiences to like the new things cinema was able to offer. But we should not equate box-office success with taste too directly. It may be that audiences did not so much like musicals *per se* as welcome the transformation in the cinematic mode of expression they ushered in. Cinema stopped trying to replicate reality in this moment of its development and began instead to consciously create its own reality. The high-gloss approach to nature one finds in contemporary cinema, which can find poetry or indeed ballet in the autumnal falling of leaves, the winterish whirl of snowflakes in the wind, or the summery dance of sunlight on water, owes its origins to this particular shifting of gears, which foregrounded colour and movement as cinematic values in their own right. These images do not merely denote seasons, they are signifiers of 'mood' – consider, by contrast, summer evoked in *Chinatown* (Polanski, 1974) and *Barton Fink* (Coen, 1991) through shots of red faces, sweating brows and peeling wallpaper, and in the background the ceaseless irritation of the whirr of a useless ceiling fan, all of which are images of heat and frustration, and the distinction soon becomes obvious.[5] If this was the historical role of the musical, then it is clearly an example of what Jameson terms a 'vanishing mediator' because the genre has almost completely disappeared from the multiplex, the few surviving examples (*Chicago* [Marshall, 2003] and *Moulin Rouge* [Luhrmann, 2001]) tending toward a kind of high seriousness completely at odds with the technicolour frivolity of their predecessors.

As Deleuze shows in his 'natural history' of cinema, which takes little notice of technological developments of any kind (with the exception of sound and colour, but even then these are treated as changes of degree not kind), the cinematic image itself changed in this period, by which he means its way of conceiving causality changed.[6] In cinema's first phase of development, which Deleuze refers to as the 'movement-image' and covers the period from the birth of cinema in 1895 to the end of World War II in 1945, causality was conceived as a 'sensory-motor' affair. The characters 'responded' to external pressures – they ran if chased, cowered if set upon, laughed or cried when stimulated to do so by the actions or words of another. The supreme moment and ultimate endpoint of this particular phase arrives with Hitchcock, who with his notorious MacGuffin (the nothing that produces something), showed that it was possible to stimulate action with merely the suggestion or illusion of a cause, mistaken identity being his prime mechanism. Hitchcock took this idea as far as it could go, Deleuze says, and his cinema marks a turning point in the development of the medium because he never figured out how to get outside this box-trap of his own making. The solution was discovered by the Italian neo-realists, Rossellini and De Sica, who in the bombed-out wastelands of post-war Europe invented a new form of 'crystalline' causality and with it a new form of image, which Deleuze dubs the 'time-image': now characters respond to what they see, and more especially what they feel, not by taking action, however, but with visions and dreams, hallucinations and madness. Something intolerable rises up within them and spills onto the screen, 'as though all the misery in the world were going to be born'.[7] This new cinema could come into being because the post-war landscape itself was already incredible, past belief, a situation for which no ready-made response existed. American directors soon followed suit, though, and the great films from this period are the ones that apprehend the new consumerist society that came into being in the post-war boom as just as alien and as much a 'destroyed' landscape as the one facing Europeans.

In a sense, then, it doesn't really matter where we begin, so long as we do not treat that starting point as in any way self-sufficient, and so long as we obey the edict to multiply the horizons in which the text is maintained and perspectives from which it is seen. Dialectical criticism sets itself apart from other kinds of criticism by the determinate way in which it develops a critique of its own concepts and categories at the same time as it deploys them. At its fullest, this means reckoning the position of the observer into the analysis and taking into account the very self-consciousness of the thinker. 'Yet self-consciousness does not mean introspection, and dialectical thinking is by no means a personal thought, but rather a way in which a certain type of material lifts itself to awareness, not only as the object of our thought, but also as a set of mental operations proposed by the intrinsic nature of that particular object' (*MF*, 341). Indeed, it may justly be said that self-consciousness of that introspective and well-nigh narcissistic type one encounters in certain of the more culturally anxious examples of cultural studies is the enemy of dialectical criticism. Painfully wrought anatomizations of one's 'privileged' speaking position (together with its *ressentiment* drenched polar opposite, the

castigation of others for their 'privileged' speaking positions) a
ema to dialectical criticism, which has always had as its goal the naming
and critiquing of the system that – among other things – seems to
demand such self-examination and indeed self-laceration. 'All thinking
about interpretation must sink itself into the strangeness, the unnatural-
ness, of the hermeneutic situation; or to put it another way, every individual interpretation must include an interpretation of its own existence,
must show its own credentials and justify itself: every commentary must
be at the same time a metacommentary as well' (*IT1*, 5). In this way,
interpretation 'directs attention back to history itself, and the historical
situation of the commentator as well as of the work' (*IT1*, 5).

Historical determinism

The question of historical determinism first raised by *Marxism and Form*
(and discussed above) is answered definitively by *The Political Unconscious*
in the long opening chapter 'On Interpretation' which we will have
occasion to return to at greater length later on (see Chapter 3). Jameson
comes at the problem via a reconsideration of the issue of causality, or
more particularly Althusser's critique of causality. For Althusser, there
are three types of causality known to epistemology, only one of which
can be considered legitimate in his view: these are (1) mechanical causality, (2) expressive causality and (3) structural causality. The first type,
mechanical causality, is, as Jameson puts it, 'exemplified in the billiard-
ball model of cause and effect' and is generally regarded as suitable only
for application in the hard or physical sciences, and then only when all
the variables and influencing factors are known and can be accounted
for ahead of time. The types and kinds of problems encountered in the
humanities are generally thought too complex for so simple a model. Yet
as Jameson reminds us, 'this type of causal analysis is by no means
everywhere discredited in cultural studies today' (*PU*, 24). He offers the
example of the history of the demise of the so-called 'triple-decker
novel' and its replacement by the cheaper one-volume format as a
case of mechanical causality at work. Writers, like George Gissing, were
suddenly compelled by force of commercial circumstance to change
the structure of their writing to accommodate this new method of
publishing – stories had to be made shorter, narrative development
compressed, all while trying to preserve the pleasure of the experience
of reading the older format (a similar story plays out in reverse in the
transition from the 'single' to the 'long-playing' record). Our discussion

above of the shift from black and white to colour film would be another equally pertinent example. 'Yet,' Jameson continues, 'what is scandalous is not this way of thinking about a given formal change, but rather the objective event itself, the very nature of cultural change in a world in which separation of use value from exchange value generates discontinuities of precisely this "scandalous" and extrinsic type' (*PU*, 26). Consequently mechanical causality can be recuperated as a symptom or effect of a social system which puts the demands and requirements of the market above everything else. In this sense, mechanical causality, used in this carefully delimited way as a means of registering the 'shocks' of a reified existence, can be salutary for cultural critics because it reminds us of the material base of cultural production.

Expressive causality is doubtless the most suspicious form of causality of them all. This, according to Althusser, is 'the model that dominates all Hegel's thought' (*PU*, 24). The problem Althusser has with it is this: 'it presupposes in principal that the whole in question be reducible to an *inner essence*, of which the elements of the whole are then no more than the phenomenal forms of expression, the inner principle of the essence being present at each point in the whole, such that at each moment it is possible to write the immediately adequate equation: such and such an element (economic, political, legal, literary, religious, etc., in Hegel) = the inner essence of the whole' (*PU*, 24). Totalization and periodization, two strategies central to Jameson's work, are both examples, or at least would be considered by Althusserians to be examples, of expressive causality, a charge Jameson readily admits, but not without insisting that it only applies to the most narrowly and poorly conceived varieties of totalization and periodization. In isolating technological development as our means of telling the history of cinema in the twentieth century, we effectively turned that into an 'inner essence' of film capable of explaining the state of the whole of the field at any one moment in its history. Shorthand references to the 'black and white period' are by this sleight of hand transformed into totalizing statements that render this moment of cinema's history as something akin to its 'long' childhood, during which it learned its craft, but only attained maturity and indeed majority with the advent of colour. Any such conception of totalization and periodization cannot escape the charge of being, as Jameson puts it, 'fatally reductive', inasmuch as it effectively constructs a one-to-one homology between available technology and creative development (*PU*, 27). So-called 'technological determinism' is simply the same argument raised to the level of the social itself. On this view of things, cultural change is in lockstep with technological change – thus it is said that the internet changed twentieth-century culture virtually overnight by dramatically increasing the speed of communication, access to information and interpersonal connectivity. All of which is undeniably true as far as it goes, but to suggest that it was the internet that caused the alleged corresponding cultural changes (for which Manuel Castells' concept of 'network society' can stand as a kind of totem) is to take no account of the vast array of other social forces operative in society at any one time. It is for this reason that Jameson has no hesitation in rejecting 'technological determinism' in all its variations as a usable means of explaining postmodernism, which is of course his own great attempt at a periodization. For Marxism, technological development is always the result or function of the development of that larger thing, namely capital itself, rather than a determining instance in its own right (*PCL*, 35).

Structural causality, the only form of causality Althusser approves of, is in Althusser's own words 'entirely summed up in the concept of "Darstellung", the key epistemological concept of the whole Marxist theory of value, the concept whose object is precisely to designate the mode of *presence* of the structure in its *effects*' (*PU*, 24). Misleadingly described as 'absent causality' because it is only visible in its effects, 'structural causality' is Spinozist in inspiration – for Spinoza, God is present everywhere and in everything because the world itself is an effect or attribute of his divine substance. Althusser's point is that the world surrounding us today is, in its every effect and attribute, from the commodities we buy to our conception of the good life, a sign of the 'divine' presence of capitalism (understood as a mode of production) as a structural cause. There is nothing 'absent' about capitalism, although from time to time we may allow it to be absent from our minds, or at least pretend to ourselves that it is. Conceived in this way, causality is no longer an inner essence concealed in an outward expression, as is the case with expressive causality, but part of the very architecture of all things. Such a system of thought would, however, soon grow too unwieldy to use because it implies that everything is not only connected to everything else, but part of the same substance. Recognizing this, and doubtlessly following Spinoza's own method of separating out the various attributes of divine substance, Althusser grants individual sections of the whole, by which he primarily means the major social institutions (or what he called the 'Ideological State Apparatuses' – schools, churches, the family, the media and so on – and the 'Repressive State Apparatuses' – the police, the military, etc.), a semi-autonomy of their own, allowing that each of these things may develop on their own and, more to the point, develop independently of, or indeed in confrontation with, some or all the other institutions. But this semi-autonomy cannot be taken to mean that one institution can be said to determine (or 'express') the whole – the whole consists in the abstract idea that holds together the multiple and differentially connected parts operating together, some-times in harmony, sometimes in conflict, to no common purpose except that of the preservation and reproduction of the system itself. 'If there-fore one wishes to characterise Althusser's Marxism as a structuralism, one must complete the characterisation with the essential proviso that it is a structuralism for which only *one* structure exists: namely the mode of production itself, or the synchronic system of social relations as a whole' (*PU*, 36).

If the different institutions in society are semi-autonomous, and no one institution can determine all the others, then if change occurs in one section, the economic sector, say, then that will not, indeed cannot, be sufficient to change the whole. By the same token, the advent of a new style of writing or way of film-making is not by itself sufficient evidence that the whole has changed. We thus come back to the issue of the proper handling of such concepts as periodization and totalization, for very clearly what is at stake here is precisely the question of just what can legitimately be used as an index of social and cultural change. Part of the answer has been given already: change occurs at the level of the whole, the abstract, or what in Marxist terminology is referred to as the mode of production, and is reflected in differing ways in the concrete institutions that comprise its actual substance. This is what Jameson means when he says his analysis of postmodernism was enabled by Ernest Mandel's *Late Capitalism* – it furnished him with a usable theor-ization of change at the level of the mode of production (*PCL*, 400). His means of tracking down change, though, is not, as it might appear, the relentless cataloguing of all the new things that are constantly being thrown up by this enormously productive global culture we know today. Although having said that, there is no one more aware of, or more sensitive to, the breadth of cultural production operative in the world today. Piling example upon example of what has been said and done takes us no nearer to an understanding of the whole, it simply gives us an accumulatively produced description which has no way of discerning in any analytically useful way what should or should not be subsumed under its categories. If every new thing is postmodern or a sign of postmodernism then that category is effectively void. Its result is that 'heap of fragments' Jameson warns us about and is no more legible to us than a pile of shoes. What one must try to do instead is triangulate what is missing, or more specifically that which could not be said, written, painted, sculpted or filmed, in our time because somehow and for reasons not disclosed it was out of step with history. Thus, as Jameson says with regards to modernism, but which we can extend to all cultural forms, our analyses need to begin with the 'taboos' each new cultural form generates as the very logic of its output, particularly those unthought (*impensé*), unsaid (*non-dit*) 'taboos' buried in the recesses of the 'political unconscious' (to use Jameson's own term) or what he also refers to as the '*pensée sauvage*' (Lévi-Strauss's term) (*PU*, 49).

Jameson's passion for Greimas's semiotic squares, which can generate a quadrant that at its limit can accommodate ten different logical relations from any starting binary pair, derives from this injunction to determine the culturally impossible. Jameson uses these squares as maps of the 'logic of closure' any concept or formal device inevitably conceals within its make-up (*FI*, xv). So, for example, as Greimas shows with respect to sexual relations, the four logical possibilities that entails (marital, normal, abnormal and extramarital) need to be seen in combination with those of rule systems (prescriptions, taboos, non-prescriptions, non-taboos), in order for us to see that 'far from designating the concrete kinship or legal systems of any specific and historical community' they are in fact nothing other than 'the empty slots and logical possibilities necessarily obtaining in all of them' (*PU*, 46). In this way, even purely formal 'impossibilities', such as the taboos on science in fantasy novels (e.g. J.R.R. Tolkien and J.K. Rowling) and relationships that do not result in marriage for romance novels (especially the Mills and Boon variety), give rise to culturally interesting questions, that is, questions that can only be answered by stepping out of the formal confines of the genre. To answer these questions we would have to determine what the positive value is in fantasy novels that cancels out the ostensive negative value of science (presumably this is magic), and then we'd want to know why this value is privileged above other possible choices (Lévi-Strauss's analyses of the *pensée sauvage* provides one possible explanation: in the magical universe there are no questions, only answers, it is thus a uniquely comforting world in contrast to the relentless questioning of the scientifistic world);[8] while for romance we would need to ascertain what negative value it is that marriage cancels out – this would yield the surprising result that 'married' is not so much the opposite of 'single' as some much more ideologically freighted notion like 'unfulfilled'.[9]

Such questions can be generated in reverse too – for instance, why did not Australia engender any authentic 'westerns' or equivalents of its own, in spite of the fact its frontier conditions and vast desert landscapes are superficially similar to the USA's? To answer this we would have to determine what positive value in the western in its US context is received as a negative, or the even more damning neither/nor value (i.e., the non-positive, non-negative, which round out the binary of positive and negative), in the Australian context – here, one suspects, it is the fact that Australia's indigenous people have never been romanticized in the same way as the indigenous peoples of North America have been that supplies the rudiments of an answer (ideologically they are typecast as children who need to be 'cared' for or, what amounts to the same thing, 'disciplined', rather than our wilder, id-like, selves represented by North America's indigenous people who need to be 'tamed').[10]

If Jameson describes his own method of dialectical criticism as the realization of Althusser's third or structural form of causality as an interpretive or hermeneutic system, then that is because what he ultimately arrives at in *The Political Unconscious* is an analytic strategy that involves 'the hypothetical *reconstruction* of the materials – content, narrative paradigms, stylistic and linguistic practices – which had to have been given in advance in order for that particular text to be produced in its unique historical specificity' (*PU*, 57–58). Dialectical criticism aims 'not so much at solving the particular dilemmas in question, as at converting those problems into their own solutions on a higher level, and making the fact and the existence of the problem itself the starting point for new research' (*MF*, 307).

Metacommentary

There is no one – or final – form of the dialectic. Therefore, there is no self-contained doctrine to go with it. Its state of being is that of antipathy and rectification, which is to say it must be defined in a twofold way: firstly in opposition to something it finds intolerable; and secondly in affirmation of a superior position it upholds as a correction of that intolerable something. So any description we give of it has to be treated like a ladder that is to be kicked away once its purpose has been served. The nearest Jameson comes to offering a template for dialectical criticism is his essay entitled 'Metacommentary', first presented at the 1971 convention of the Modern Language Association, where, as it happens, it was awarded the association's William Riley Parker Prize. In typical fashion, he approaches the general theoretical problem that concerns him via a confrontation with a contemporary 'false' problem, in this case the alleged 'end of interpretation', or more specifically the 'end of content', the former being conditional on the latter, that we associate with Susan Sontag's influential 1965 essay 'Against Interpretation', which as Jameson points out was only the latest permutation of this critical turn. All the great schools of thought that shaped twentieth-century literary and philosophical thinking, from logical positivism and pragmatism through to existentialism, Russian Formalism and structuralism, 'share a renunciation of *content*' and 'find their fulfilment in formalism, in the refusal of all presuppositions about substance and human nature, and in the substitution of method for metaphysical system' (*IT1*, 3). Content varies in definition according to the historical situation, but at base always implies some extra-semantic conception of meaning – the notion of 'symbol' is exemplary in this respect – in which the meaning of a word or image is independent of form and in a certain sense superior to it as well.[11] T.S. Eliot's 'hollow men' and Joseph Conrad's 'heart of darkness' are among the more well-known instances of this phenomenon. By contrast, Sontag and others (notably Ihab Hassan and Jean-François Lyotard), would urge the critic to look for the paradoxical presence of the inexpressible in texts and tended to favour those works which seemed pregnant with silence – or, 'difficult', in the language of the period – rather than full of meaning.

Thus Sontag would write:

> In the strictest sense, all the contents of consciousness are ineffable. Even the simplest sensation is, in its totality, indescribable. Every work of art, therefore, needs to be understood not only as something rendered, but also as a certain handling of the ineffable. In the greatest art, one is always aware of things that cannot be said (rules of 'decorum'), of the contradiction between expression and the presence of the inexpressible. Stylistic devices are also techniques of avoidance. The most potent elements in a work of art are, often, its silences.[12]

Jameson does not respond directly to the strong and often heated denunciations of the practice of textual criticism embodied in the anti-interpretive position by trying to argue for the continuing possibility and indeed necessity of interpretation as many of his colleagues tried, and largely failed, to do in this period, which we now look back on, in the manner of a science fiction novel, as the first of the 'theory wars'. The scorched-earth rhetoric adhered to by the original exponents of deconstruction (Jacques Derrida, Paul De Man, J. Hillis Miller and Geoffrey Hartman) as it was trying to establish itself as *the* model of literary criticism in the 1970s left a blazing trail of victims (most famously J.R. Searle and M.H. Abrams) behind it as it worked its way critically through all the 'old' methods and practices of doing textual criticism, invariably finding them ontologically wanting for not realizing the sheer impossibility of what they thought they were doing. It is impossible to find *the* meaning of any text, deconstruction insists, because the very search for meaning is in itself productive of meaning, so the more diligently one interprets a text the more impossible it becomes to actually bring the process to a halt and stop at some final or ultimate point of meaning-fulness, except to conclude as deconstruction rather truculently does that the final result must be an 'undecidable'.[13] Jameson's response to these debates has been to stage a threefold reversal: (1) at the local level, that of the highly routinized practice of interpreting texts, Jameson argues that there is no need to interpret texts (not that it is impossible to do so) because they come to us as already interpreted; (2) at the wider level of how one should go about interpreting texts and indeed the question of whether it is even possible to do so, Jameson argues that this question is always decided in advance in the logic of the mode of criticism itself, therefore the important question is not how one should interpret a text but why one would want to do so in the first place; and (3) at the level of discourse, or of the social itself, he argues that both these questions need to be re-examined from the perspective of their historical necessity – why is it, in other words, that one kind of critical practice is able to triumph at another's expense? Taken together, these three propositions constitute the basic fabric or essential matrix (in Žižek's sense) of the method Jameson provisionally termed 'metacommentary'.

The first proposition, that texts do not need to be interpreted because they are already interpreted, is argued for in the following way: the raw material of texts, what is usually called 'content', is 'never initially form-less, never, like the unshaped substances of the other arts, initially con-tingent, but rather is itself already meaningful from the outset, being nothing more nor less than the very components of our concrete social life: words, thoughts, objects, desires, people, places, activities' (*IT1*, 14). The work of art does not make these things meaningful – they are already meaningful – but rather transforms their meaning, or else rearranges them in such a way as to heighten and intensify their mean-ingfulness. This process is not arbitrary, however, but follows an inner logic that can be abstracted, which is to say thought about and con-sidered independently of the text itself. Jameson's hypothesis is that this logic takes the form of a censorship, the internally consistent and inwardly felt need to not say some things and to try to say other things in their place. Metacommentary 'implies a model not unlike the Freudian hermeneutic (divested, to be sure, of its own specific content, of the topology of the unconscious, the nature of the libido, and so forth), one based on the distinction between symptom and repressed idea, between manifest and latent content, between the message and the message disguised' (*IT1*, 13). This image can stand as shorthand for what it is the metacommentary does, provided it is understood that the object of the game is not to redeem or restore the suppressed content, but to uncover the logic of that suppression. As Žižek helpfully reminds us, the structure of Freud's interpretative model is in fact triple not double as is commonly assumed: its three operative elements are (1) the manifest content, (2) the latent content and (3) unconscious desire. 'This desire attaches itself to the dream, it intercalates itself in the interspace between the latent thought and the manifest content; it is therefore not "more concealed" in relation to the latent thought, it is decidedly more "on the surface", consisting entirely of the signifier's mechanisms, of the treatment to which the latent thought is submitted. In other words, its only place is in the *form* of the "dream": the real subject matter of the dream (the unconscious desire) articulates itself in the dream-work, in the elaboration of its "latent content" ' (*SO*, 13). Not only is the manifest content already meaningful, so is the latent content too – indeed, if this were not the case, the entire Freudian hermeneutic would be disabled.

Psychoanalysis works because we know (or stipulate) that everything in the dream stands for sex (the primal scene). In practice, then, psychoanalysis *never* asks what the dream means because it knows the answer to that already. What it wants to know is how and why the dream-work managed to transform the dream-thought into *that*! The shock of psychoanalysis does not arise from the insight that sometimes a cigar stands for a penis, but rather the opposite thought that sometimes penis can be represented as a cigar, or more to the point, that sometimes a penis *needs* to be represented as a cigar so that we can properly understand its significance to the matrix of our unconscious desire. The intriguing interpretive questions that arise from this observation have to do with the personal associations we make in connection with cigars (these could come from television, magazines or personal experience), their actual physical properties, such as their shape, as well as any practical experience we might have with them (obviously their fundamentally oral nature is pertinent, but so too their combustibility). It follows, then, that the essential dialectical question is not what has been repressed in the course of the writing process, although that is important, nor why it is repressed, though that is important too, but rather how does that repression work. The cognate concepts of the 'political unconscious', '*pensée sauvage*', as well as the later notion of 'cultural logic', all refer essentially to this process and not, it must be added, to some secret reservoir of meanings buried deep in the text. In answer to the 'why' question, which as we have said is important without being decisive, Jameson finds a great deal to interest him in Freud's short paper of 1908, 'Creative Writers and Day-Dreaming' (*PU*, 175; *IT1*, 76–77; *AF*, 45–47). Freud's basic argument is that other people's fantasies – including fetishes and obsessions – when communicated in their raw form are actually kind of boring and even a little repellent (this is true even for the psychoanalyst whose job often consists in nothing more than listening to precisely such boring and repellent stories). If the writer does not want to put us off – if, in other words, they are to take proper notice of their audience – then they have to find a way of disguising their fetishes and giving them another form. This, Freud suggests, is the basic task of aesthetics, and our pleasure in reading derives from our appreciation of the skill the writer exercises in keeping their text free from embarrassingly 'personal' elements all the while giving us access to the full power of their imagination. We want orcs and goblins and elves, not the private dreams and petty anxieties of a South African-born Oxford don, and doubtless that is one of the reasons why Tolkien's work is so enduringly popular.[14]

As Jameson observes in his seminal 1978 essay on psychoanalysis, 'Imaginary and Symbolic in Lacan', what is problematical about psychoanalytic criticism is not its insistence on the presence of 'Oedipal' complexes, but rather its failure to pay attention to 'the transformational process whereby such private materials become public' (*IT1*, 76). Jameson proposes that this transformational process, aestheticization process, as we might more properly call it, whereby the writer renders their private fancies publicly acceptable can be understood in terms of Freud's analyses of the function of dream-work. According to Freud, the dream-work has two techniques at its disposal for transforming the prohibited dream-thoughts from their raw unacceptable state into their highly mediated or overwritten acceptable state. These are the processes of displacement and condensation which, as Lacan demonstrated are comparable to the rhetorical tropes of metaphor and metonymy. These processes reveal their presence in symptoms, most notably when our reaction to a thought, idea, action or image is disproportionate to the surface content of it. We might jump in fright at the sight of a tiny spider, even though we are not really afraid of spiders, because somehow a nameless anxiety we were feeling in relation to something else, but had not yet confronted head on, is displaced onto the spider, making it the vehicle for the anxiety rather than the actual object cause of it. Similarly, when our partner forgets to take out the trash or put their clothes away these trivial sins of omission might evoke a powerfully angry response on our part, but not because we care so much about whether the trash was put out or not, but because in this one act is condensed, or telescoped, all the other gripes we might have boiling up inside us.

Freud's account of the aestheticization process exhibits these same two processes at work: 'gratification of the wish by its displacement and disguise', on the one hand, and 'a simultaneous release of psychic energy owing to the formal shortcuts and superpositions' (*IT1*, 77) of condensation, on the other. 'Flaubert's program for the depersonalisation of the literary text can thus in one way be seen as the recognition of the dilemma designated by Freud, and as the systematic attempt to remove all traces of wish-fulfilment from the narrative surface' (*PU*, 175). Yet it is also obvious that the concepts of displacement and condensation are ultimately useless to us past the point of explaining how a certain private wish achieved its public face because they cannot explain why a writer should choose to censor the products of their imagination in the particular way that they do – why orcs, goblins and elves and not some other set of magical creatures, and indeed why use the fantasy tropes at all?

We cannot answer this question without first determining the nature of the repressed message itself, which for Jameson is not a matter of private fantasies and fetishes, but rather the public – that is to say, collective – anxiety of the nature and quality of lived experience itself for which the shorthand 'history' serves duty to refer to throughout Jameson's work. Private fantasies and fetishes are simply symptomal responses to the deeper realities of what has been described above as the mode of production and need to be interpreted in terms of the privations of history rather than the psychopathologies of sexual dysfunction. More pointedly, they express in their own perverse way a longing for an altered 'form of life', one in which certain satisfactions are readily supplied and do not suffer the proscriptions of our own moralizing universe, and can in this sense be seen as utopian.

> Yet the content of such experience can never be determined in advance, and varies from the most grandiose forms of action to the most minute and limited feelings and perceptions in which consciousness can be specialised. It is easier to express the properties of this phenomenon negatively, by saying that the idea of Experience

always presupposes its opposite, that is, a kind of life that is mere vegetation, that is routine, emptiness, passage of time. (*IT1*, 16)

The work of art juxtaposes the representation of a lived experience as its basic content with an implied question as to the very possibility of a meaningful experience as its form. 'It thereby obeys a double impulse. On the one hand, it preserves the subject's fitful contact with genuine life and serves as the repository for that mutilated fragment of Experience which is her treasure, or his. Meanwhile, its mechanisms function as a censorship, which secures the subject against awareness of the resulting impoverishment, while preventing him/her from identifying connections between that impoverishment and mutilation and the social system itself' (*IT1*, 16). The ultimate obscenity, and that which we must try to find the means of coming to terms with, is history itself, but not the dry and lifeless catalogue of 'facts' and spurious narratives we encounter in textbooks. History, for Jameson, is a living thing, and it is the task of critics to show how its beating heart animates *all* forms of cultural production.

The writer's two problems

This task is difficult (as we will explore in more detail in Chapter 3), because in contrast to psychoanalysis, say, we cannot stipulate in advance what the repressed content of history will look like, save that it must have to do with class conflict. Jameson's solution to this interpretive problem, adapted largely from Russian Formalism, but modified so as to factor a consideration of history into it, is to reverse the very terms of the problem itself and stop seeing it from the critic's point of view and look at it instead from the writer's point of view and thereby try to see how these demands are met and dealt with in practical terms. By effectively turning the work inside out, the Russian Formalists were able to dispose of a number of false problems of the thematic variety, such as whether or not Gogol should be considered a 'romantic', or Don Quixote a myth: the aim of the artist is ultimately, and in a real sense *only*, to produce the work itself. On Russian Formalism's view of things, it was because Gogol wished 'to work in a particular kind of form, and to speak in the tone of voice of the *skaz*, that he casts about for raw materials appropriate to it, for anecdotes, names, piquant details, sudden shifts in manner' (*IT1*, 7). By the same token: 'Don Quixote is not really a character at all, but rather an organisational device that permits Cervantes to write his book, serving as a thread that holds a number of different types of anecdotes together in a single form. (Thus Hamlet's madness permitted Shakespeare to piece together several heterogeneous plot sources, and Goethe's Faust is an excuse for the dramatisation of many different moods)' (*IT1*, 7). Perhaps the keenest articulation of this approach, and certainly the one that – in my case at least – produces the 'shock' proper to dialectical criticism, is Jameson's *tour de force* analysis of Ernest Hemingway's style. 'Hemingway's great discovery', Jameson suggests, 'was that there was possible a kind of return to the very sources of verbal productivity if you forgot about words entirely and merely concentrated on prearranging the objects that the words were supposed to describe' (*MF*, 410). The real event of Hemingway's work, for both author and reader alike, is the production of the sentences themselves and what we read him for, finally, is not the content of his novels – the shooting of an elephant say, or the death-dance of the bullfight – but to see whether his sentences will prove adequate to the occasion.

The first problem a writer has to confront therefore is nothing other than the problem of how to get started. Hemingway's great discovery, that if he arranged objects and let words follow, is in effect nothing other than Hemingway's own solution to this particular problem. He would leave things out. It may be this brute fact of its production that gives the work its constitutive 'ugliness', an idea Jameson takes from Gertrude Stein and uses in a number of places to characterize what it is that the critic is trying to recapture by thinking about the way the work got made (*WS*, 11). Let me give another example of this approach from Jameson's work, this time his essay on Wallace Stevens.

> In Stevens, the place-name will be at one and the same time the very locus and occasion for a production of images: quasi-Flaubertian *bovarysme*, the daydream about the exotic place, the free association on Java, Tehentepec, Key West, Oklahoma, Tennessee, Yucatan, Carolina, and so forth – and the emergence of another level of systematicity in language itself (the generation of place-names out of each other, their association now as a proper vocabulary field), behind which a deeper system is concealed and active. (*WS*, 14)

That deeper system is the exoticism of the Third World. The point, though, is not to accuse Stevens of orientalism (though it should not thereby be seen to excuse him of it either), but to show the degree to which the exoticism of the Third World is in some way structurally required by the work itself. As Jameson reads it, the so-called Third World material in Stevens' work (his casual references to Java and so forth) is not merely the private fantasy of someone who did not travel all that much but nevertheless longed to somehow escape his own skin, although it is certainly that too, but the content his chosen form demanded (*WS*, 15). Put simply, the everyday imagery in Stevens which constantly risks falling into a dreary realism, the sheerest chattering of commodities, is saved from this fate of banality by its juxtaposition with geographical otherness, '*Java* tea' being more intriguing to the stifled minds of consumer society than 'tea' by itself, something we can be sure a poet so well acquainted with advertising as Stevens could hardly escape noticing. Similarly, Jameson reads Rimbaud's well-nigh hallucinogenic references to 'Africa the Far East, a delirious tropics, a phantasmagorical Germany' (*RS*, 71) in much the same way, as that 'exotic' content which is structurally required by the form in order to get started. In explanation of this, Jameson offers up the delicious idea of a 'geographical Unconscious' which he explicitly links to Stevens, but alas has not developed any further elsewhere in his work (although it shows an obvious affinity with his concept of 'Cognitive Mapping').

Sentences do not fall ready-made from the sky, they require a type-specific machine to get them going. Often this takes the form of an obstacle or taboo, such as Joyce's self-imposed rule in *Ulysses* to try to capture everything, right down to the most banal detail. Once in progress, though, sentence production becomes a kind of limitlessness, an inexhaustible energy, an unstoppable productivity, like desire itself (in Deleuze and Guattari's terms), that could never be constrained enough for meaning to exist were there not a countervailing force at work, and this is precisely how contradiction is to be understood in the literary critical setting. The writer's second problem, then, is the opposite of the first, and that is the problem of closure: all writers must confront the question of how to bring closure to their work that is not a purely arbitrary cut-off, or stopping point, but has some kind of internally consistent and indeed viscerally felt necessity. Jameson's prime exhibit in this respect is Joyce (*U*, *MI*). What we must do in the case of Joyce's *Ulysses* Jameson argues is historicize its very form, which in this case means explaining its adoption of the structure of Homer's mythic tale of the exploits of Odysseus. In effect, this means setting aside the idea that the mythic structure itself is the source of meaning.[15] Having decided to start his writing by trying to note down all the experiences of a single day, interior and exterior, but in such a way as to register the fragmenting effect of modern life itself, which is essentially the life of the industrial city, Joyce's text is soon overwhelmed with detail. At every turn it risks shattering into the merely fragmented – a catalogue of walks taken at lunchtime, buying cakes of soap, billboards, idle thoughts, dirty thoughts and so on. Each of these fragments being, as Jameson puts it, 'infinitely subdivisible', there is nothing to say that 'the transformation of these segments into narrative sentences might not be infinitely extended and indeed last forever. The Odyssey parallel helps avoid this unwelcome development and sets just such external limits, which ultimately become those of Joyce's minimal units of composition – the individual chapters themselves' (*U*, 132). The mythic framework does not so much confer meaning on the whole as save it from sliding into a kind of pointless chattering (Franco Moretti provocatively, but accurately one feels, describes the experience of reading *Ulysses* as being like listening to the radio, presumably set to some all-day chat show).[16] Sheer sentence production is literally schizophrenic, a private madness no reader could ever fully participate in. What the mythic framework does is provide an instrument or machine – borrowing from Lyotard, Jameson calls it a 'libidinal apparatus' (*FA*, 10) – that, operating at a collective level, enables readers to 'invest' in the text.

Jameson's most fully developed treatment on this strategy of analyzing texts in terms of what I have been calling the writer's two problems is *Fables of Aggression*, a book that takes up the challenge of writing sympathetically about the politically discredited modernist author Wyndham Lewis, who late in life expressed an unfortunate enthusiasm for fascism. Jameson's interest in Lewis certainly does not stem from any particular sympathy for his politics, which in addition to fascism also encompassed a virulent anti-communism and an abiding misogyny. To his credit, however, Lewis was 'an internationalist, the most European and least insular of all the great contemporary British writers' (*FA*, 88). It is Lewis's style that captivates Jameson:

> To face the sentences of Wyndham Lewis is to find oneself confronted with a principle of immense mechanical energy. Flaubert, *Ulysses*, are composed; the voices of a James or of a Faulkner develop their resources through some patient blind groping exploration of their personal idiosyncrasies from work to work. The style of Lewis, however, equally unmistakable, blasts through the tissues of his novels like a steam whistle, breaking them to its will. (*FA*, 25)

Given what we have said above about the constant risk of disintegrating into an almanac of unrelated facts of both the historical and anecdotal kind Joyce's work seems to court, probably the most startling claim in the preceding quotation is that *Ulysses* is a highly composed work, the implication being that its riskiness is more apparent than real. And indeed this is precisely what Jameson does suggest. Far 'from dissolving the personality into its external determinations', namely the relentless chattering of the city from its endless signage to countless overheard conversations on buses and trains, 'the Joycean phantasmagoria serves to reconfirm the unity of the psyche, and to reinvent that depth-psychological perspective from which these fantasies spring' (*FA*, 57). But what is more significant, Jameson continues, is the way Joyce's sentences are coordinated by the larger but 'absent' structure of the mythic framework, which he suggests functions to remind us that the present is riven by repetition, much in the same way as Freud's notion of the uncanny does. This insight into Joyce gives us a clue as to how Lewis contains his own much less composed – it would be wrong to describe them as discomposing – grinding sentences. He too must deploy some kind of framework to impose a logic of closure on his unruly texts, but in contrast to Joyce who retains the individual consciousness as his basic point of reference Lewis explodes even that safety net, making the Homeric universe, ruled as it is by self-enclosed actors, unsuited to his purposes. His model is the nation-state system and the result something Jameson terms 'national allegory'.

> This account of the preconditions of Lewis' novel is a very different proposition from interpretive statements which might take it as the 'reflexion' of the European diplomatic system or see its violent content as betraying some 'homology' with World War I. An analysis of the semantic and structural preconditions of a form is not a correspondence theory of art; nor do we mean to see national allegory as an afterimage given off by the international diplomatic system itself. Rather, like any form, it must be read as an instable and provisory solution to an aesthetic dilemma which is itself the manifestation of a social and historical contradiction. (*FA*, 94)

There is no more misunderstood term in all of Jameson's many conceptual coinages than this one, 'national allegory', which was passed over largely unremarked in its first flush in *Fables of Aggression* but came to enjoy something approaching notoriety after its second airing in the 1986 essay, 'Third-World Literature in the Era of Multinational Capitalism'.[17] Here, though, we are concerned only with the question of how this concept works. The idea behind it stems from the observation that Freud's work is enabled by 'preexisting representations of the topography of the city and the dynamics of the political state [e.g., the topography of the unconscious, the economics of the ego, and the energy model of the death wish]. This urban and civil "apparatus" – often loosely referred to as a Freudian "metaphor" – is the objective precondition for Freud's representation of the psyche, and is thus at one with the very "discovery" of the unconscious itself, which may now be seen to have presupposed the objective development – the industrialisation, the social stratification and class polarisation, the complex division of labour – of the late Victorian city' (*FA*, 96). The nation-state system is the objective precondition of Lewis's work. What it presents is a model of virtual stability, or perhaps it would be better to say a model of stability in the virtual realm of the idea of the nation, that is able to contain a riot of actual instability, which is to say the instability of the actual itself caught in the ceaseless flow of time. This is effectively what Benedict Anderson means to suggest with his conception of nation as an 'imagined community', an idea that in his later work on globalization Jameson would find usefully suggestive.[18] In this sense, it is not merely a formal solution to a sheerly formal problem, it is also an attempt to use history homeopathically, that is to say it is an attempt to use history to solve the existential crises and dilemmas history itself throws up.[19]

> Thus, national allegory should be understood as a formal attempt to bridge the increasing gap between the existential data of everyday life within a given nation-state and the structural tendency of monopoly capital to develop on a worldwide, essentially transnational scale. Nineteenth-century or 'classical' realism presupposed the relative intelligibility and self-sufficiency of the national experience from within, a coherence in its social life such that the narrative of the destinies of its individual citizens can be expected to achieve formal completeness. (*FA*, 94)

This expectation was dashed by the catastrophe that was World War I and with it this particular formal solution.

Dialectical criticism and utopia

In *The Political Unconscious* Jameson brings the whole issue of the existence and necessity of interpretation to a determinate end. Interpretation exists, he argues, because society is not transparent, the workings of power are not always obvious, and we have a corresponding need to decipher the mysterious fabric of our existence (*PU*, 60–61). As we will see more clearly in the next chapter and those that follow, it is the central task of dialectical criticism to keep alive the possibility of praxis by making the present thinkable and by sustaining our collective faith in the utopian idea that the future is always open and that cataclysm and disaster are not the only ways for us to imagine change. The 'dialectic is not a thing of the past', Jameson insists, 'but rather a speculative account of some thinking of the future which has not yet been realised: an unfinished project, as Habermas might put it; a way of grasping situations and events that does not yet exist as a collective habit because the concrete form of social life to which it corresponds has not yet come into being' (*PD*, 359).

Notes

1　As we will see in Chapter 3, *The Political Unconscious* is the formal realization of this demand.
2　See P. Wollen, *Readings and Writings* (London: Verso, 1982). For Jameson's own consideration of film stock see *SV*, 143, 180.
3　Today this story could be told in terms of the decision to use CGI – with CGI film can tell virtually any kind of story it wants to, but this freedom of content comes at the price of an enormous increase in production costs. As with the introduction of colour, which was also comparatively expensive, an increase in production cost demands an increase in returns at the box-office and this in turn leads to the star system (a marketing solution above all else), but also a compromise in narrative since the film must now strive for maximum appeal. So at the moment of the highest technical freedom, film narrative knows its greatest level of constraint: its stars will only appear in a very limited range of roles (Julia Roberts will never play a truly 'evil' character) and its stories must cut across the maximum number of demographics (i.e., put off the least amount of people).
4　For Jameson (*MA*, 238), then, this is the effect of Virilio's decision to base his histories on such single-dimensional categories as speed.
5　For a marvellous discussion of the affect of heat in science fiction see *AF*, 268–70.
6　G. Deleuze, *Cinema 2: The Time-Image* (trans. H. Tomlinson and R. Galeta; Minneapolis: University of Minnesota Press, 1989) pp. 1–24.
7　Ibid.
8　C. Lévi-Strauss, *The Savage Mind* (Chicago: Chicago University Press, 1966) p. 22.
9　As evidence we might point to the way, in Britain at least, the early publicity for a Viagra for women (PT–141) has been met with the 'concern' that it will lead to an increase in 'emotionally malnourished' sex, or what one wit has labelled 'McNookie'.

10 I hope it is clear that 'care' here is an ideologically loaded term, one that has in the past, and still today, licensed a great many of the actions taken against the indigenous people of Australia (the 'Stolen Generation' being only the most well-known example).

11 On the difference between symbol, metaphor and allegory, see *FMA*.

12 S. Sontag, *Against Interpretation* (London: Vintage, 2001) p. 36.

13 This is not necessarily a bad thing, as Jameson has remarked (in a different context), 'provided we continue to try to decide' whatever it is that has been declared 'undecidable' (*AF*, xiv).

14 Jameson (*GAH*, 186) deploys this thesis to explain the repugnance we feel in the face of James Dickey's novel *Deliverance*.

15 Even more provocatively, Jameson (*DD*, 218) extends this idea to a reading of *Dekalog* (Kieślowski, 1988).

16 F. Moretti, *Modern Epic: The World System from Goethe to García Márquez* (trans. Q. Hoare; London: Verso, 1996) p. 142.

17 I deal with the 'notoriety' this concept attracted and the misunderstandings it occasioned in I. Buchanan, 'National Allegory Today – A Return to Jameson', in C. Irr and I. Buchanan (eds), *On Jameson: From Postmodernism to Globalisation* (New York: SUNY Press, 2006) pp. 173–88. For an affirmative account of how this concept might productively be used for postcolonial critical purposes see I. Szeman, *Zones of Instability: Literature, Postcolonialism, and the Nation* (Baltimore: Johns Hopkins University Press, 2003).

18 B. Anderson, *Imagined Communities: Reflections on the Origins and Spread of Nationalism* (London: Verso, 1983).

19 This notion of homeopathy derives from *RP*, 59–60; *PCL*, 409.

Chapter 2

Sartre, Adorno, Brecht and Barthes

> I have felt that the dialectical method can be acquired only by a concrete working through of detail, by a sympathetic internal experience of the gradual construction of a system according to its inner necessity.
>
> Fredric Jameson, *Marxism and Form*

In the introduction to *Marxism and Form* and in a number of his interviews, Jameson acknowledges the importance of a number of thinkers in the development of his own work and indeed of his own intellectual formation. Four in particular stand out as having been crucial: Sartre, Adorno, Brecht and Barthes. He has written about many other theorists besides these four and it is obvious, too, that he profits from encounters with a huge range of thinkers other than these four, including some such as Heidegger and Luhmann who he does not regard as politically congenial. A short list of the more important of these intellectual interlocutors would include Baudrillard, Benjamin, Bloch, Deleuze, Freud, Greimas, Lacan, Lefebvre, Lukács, Lyotard and Marin. However none of these others seem to have had quite the same formative effect on his method as Sartre, Adorno, Brecht and Barthes. Here I am drawing a distinction (along the lines of Hjelmslev's division between the form of content and the form of expression) between the matrix of Jameson's method (form of content), which we've already identified as the metacommentary, and the compendium of concepts the matrix is capable of absorbing and turning to its own purpose (content of the form). Taking what is undoubtedly the most visible of such concepts, namely Greimas's semiotic square, it is clear that the metacommentary can use Greimas's concept for its own purposes, but the square is not instrumental to the formation of the method. Extending this same claim to Lacan or Lukács, say, would obviously be more controversial, but no less instructive: Jameson makes use of Lacan (as well as Freud of course), but always with the proviso that the content of his theory be x-rayed out, leaving behind a stripped-down apparatus freed from its doctrine; similarly, he readily deploys Lukács's notion of form, but sets aside its political baggage (e.g., Lukács's commitment to Stalinism and so forth, about which Jameson says, with considerable sympathy for the writer's situation, that it 'was required for the public participation in the debates of the party intellectuals' [*IFJ*, 78]). Having examined the metacommentary at length in the previous chapter, here I want to review the critical spadework that went on behind the scenes, 'the sympathetic internal experience' mentioned above, that led first of all to the formation of the method itself and subsequently fuelled its refinement and expansion.

This labour encompasses the full spectrum of Jameson's career – his book on Sartre, which also happens to be his first publication, was published in 1961, and came from his PhD completed at Yale in 1959; while the book on Brecht was written for the latter's centenary four decades later in 1998. Theory as we know it today did not exist when Jameson was doing his PhD, which he thought of as an exercise in what was then known as 'style studies' (see the interview in this volume). The Sartre of his PhD, however, is not the Sartre of *Marxism and Form*. Gone is the analysis of how Sartre wrote certain of his texts, and in its place is a detailed examination of Sartre's method for reading texts. This shift in perspective from content or style to method encapsulates the transformation in literary studies that in the last decades of the twentieth century gave rise to what we know today as theory. Perhaps uniquely, Jameson is at once historian, critic and contributor to this movement. One can read his author studies, then, developed as they were at irregular intervals throughout his entire career, in both book and essay form, as milestones on the road to the invention of theory. It is clear by 1998 when the book on Brecht appears that not only does theory exist in its 'full-blown' form it has started to splinter and fragment, suggesting a new age is almost upon us. At a conference held in December 2001 in Hobart, at the University of Tasmania (Australia), pointedly titled 'What's Left of Theory?', Jameson did in fact suggest something like this, although he stopped short of saying what this new era would look like, save that he thought it might see the revival of the dialectic's fortunes.[1] Ultimately, as was made clear in the talk, Jameson is ambivalent about theory – its strength, as he sees it, is that it is better equipped to deal with the complexities of a globalized world than philosophy, which is constrained (at least in its Anglo-American or analytic modes) by its search for the universal and the singular and the need to conceive closed systems of thought; he is even prepared to entertain the idea that contemporary art, from Wallace Stevens on he suggests, requires theory as an essential resource to give meaning to its experimentations; but he deplores its optionality, its lack of a committed politics, and the egotism of thinking that its reading is a kind of writing.[2]

If one reads Jameson's writings as he reads Adorno's in *Late Marxism*, 'synchronously, as parts of a single unfolding system' (*LM*, 3), then Sartre, Adorno, Brecht and Barthes, appear and reappear like characters in Honoré de Balzac's *Comédie Humaine* – as is the case in Balzac's masterpiece, different books focus on different characters, giving them greater or lesser prominence according to the particular demands of the drama, but none of the characters either dominate the drama as a whole or ever fully recede from view, and most have small parts to play outside their own stories. More particularly, though, what I want to show here is the strategic importance of these portraits. They are a crucial part of Jameson's life-long campaign to not only argue for a Marxist viewpoint of the world, but to popularize it as well. Sartre, Adorno, Brecht and Barthes are complex, ambivalent, idiosyncratic and problematic heroes of the Left held before us not as idols to emulate but rather as figures who make us think, and whose very existence goes a long way toward undermining the 'Washington Consensus' that there is only one way of thinking about the world. Another world is not merely possible, it already exists.

Sartre

A 'book of philosophy is also a language experiment' (*S*, 67). In this fragment of a sentence we witness the genesis of what we know to be Jameson's method, namely the metacommentary. Thus the Sartre of Jameson's style-studies period is already well on the way to becoming the Sartre of *Marxism and Form*, where Jameson acknowledges that although he has reservations about stylistics as a method, he remains 'faithful to the notion that any concrete description of a literary or philosophical phenomenon – if it is to be really complete – has an ultimate obligation to come to terms with the shape of the individual sentences themselves, to give an account of their origin and formation' (*MF*, xii). The book on Sartre was where Jameson learned how to do this and *Marxism and Form* was where he showed how this fine-grained reading of a text went hand in hand with politics. So while it is true that what results is the magical appearance of two Sartres, it is an optical illusion.

What changes between times is Jameson's situation, to use an apposite

Sartrean concept. The first Sartre is that of a graduate student living and working in Boston and studying at Yale in a time of economic prosperity and 'Cold War'. The latter is that of an associate professor who has left his Ivy League beginnings behind for the brave new world of a new university in San Diego, California in a time of intense domestic unrest and a 'Hot War' in Vietnam.[3] This transformation is registered in the introduction to *Marxism and Form*, where he writes of a global situation defined by 'neocolonialism, oppression, and counter-insurgency warfare' (*MF*, xviii). Acutely aware of his own national situation, Jameson acknowledges that the US experience of war, in contrast to Europe's, is indirect and 'entangled in the sticky cobwebs of the false and unreal culture' (*MF*, xviii) of what he would later term postmodernism. In other words, Jameson does not buy into the widely held idea that Sartre's career falls into two halves, divided by the appearance of the *Critique of Dialectical Reason*. He takes the view that this division, which is obviously self-serving inasmuch as it gives the critic an excuse to search for inconsistencies between the two moments of Sartre's career, is static and unhelpful. It is 'more satisfactory', he argues, 'to think that the *Critique* comes to complete *Being and Nothingness* in certain basic areas where it remained abstract or insufficiently developed; and that this act of completion, lifting all the problems onto a higher dialectical plane, ends by utterly transforming the very appearance of the earlier system' (*MF*, 209).

In his own career, the Sartre book, as is the case for so many PhDs, has been something of a 'vanishing mediator' – it is given remarkably short shrift in most accounts of his work, yet, as I am insisting here, it is central to the formation of his method.[4] As one expects of a dissertation, it has an intense, almost forensic, fascination for its own subject matter, which it conceives as a very select and quite distinctive set of problems in Sartre's style. There is virtually no mention of Sartre's politics, his involvement in various anti-war movements, his support for Algerian nationalism, student radicalism, Simone de Beauvoir, his dispute with Albert Camus, nor any of the other familiar biographical vignettes and motifs of Sartre the 'public intellectual'. The book is, in this sense, quite unworldly, but no more so than, say, Edward Said's PhD, *Joseph Conrad and the Fiction of Autobiography*. I would venture to say that it is only *too unworldly* in the author's own eyes. At least this is the impression one gets from his 1984 afterword which, with evident embarrassment, describes the work as impressionistic and intuitive and offers to rewrite it in a 'more satisfactory terminology' (*S*, 205), meaning the critical vernacular of theory. The afterword is additionally noteworthy for the appeal it makes to Walter Benjamin's conception of historicism, which is strong and direct enough to suggest he could be considered a fifth actor in this four-handed drama. Benjamin's work is used as a kind of magnifying lens; it makes visible in a properly historical fashion what were previously only the insights of a sympathetic and indeed empathetic fellow writer. Jameson's later work on Sartre will give us the expected portrait of a committed intellectual acting out his political convictions on a world stage. In 'Periodizing the 60s', published in the same year as the afterword, Jameson describes Sartre as 'one of the last great system builders of philosophy', positioning him as the thinker of our time who showed us – as much by the failure of his grandest project, namely the unfinished *Critique*, to reach its appointed terminus, as by his many notable successes – the structural limits of philosophy in a period of world history no longer amenable to its systemic approach (*IT2*, 187).

Perhaps the most famous definition of style is Marcel Proust's luminous idea that having a style means making a foreign language out of one's own language. It is the literary equivalent of speaking in tongues. Style is certainly one of the slipperier notions literary criticism has invented as a way of distinguishing between works, both within the oeuvre of a single author, and between the oeuvres of several authors. Style is what authors acquire in their maturity, it is often said. It is also a métier, a way of doing things with words peculiar to the author. It appears at the most microscopic of levels – the placement of commas, the use of periods, semicolons and so forth, but also the choice of words (what poets refer to as 'language'), sentence types, paragraphing, all the way up to choice of subject matter and imagery. Style separates the Joyce of *Portrait of the Artist as a Young Man* from the Joyce of *Ulysses* and the Joyce of *Finnegans Wake* and for many Joyce is not really Joyce until he discovers his style. Before then he is just one among many struggling artists and wannabe authors. The essential proposition of style studies is, as Jameson observes in the opening sentence of *Sartre: The Origins of a Style*, that style 'is somehow in itself intelligible, above and beyond the limited meaning of the book written in it, and beyond even those precise meanings which the individual sentences that make it up appear to convey' (*S*, vii).

Style is intrinsic to the very construction of the text, governing every detail of it from the smallest to the largest, yet at the same time somehow extrinsic to it as well, available for inspection and interrogation in its own right. One has constantly to imagine as an ongoing thought-experiment that somehow the text before us might have been written differently, that deliberate and isolable choices were made that resulted in this specific assemblage of words, sentences and paragraphs. But to understand this process properly one has also to come to grips with the text's constraints too, that which it somehow had no choice but finally to do. In other words style is not an exercise in pure optionality – the artist does not have complete freedom: he or she is constrained by both the matter they are forced to work with and the audience they are trying to speak to. Creativity, then, is what one has when one figures out how to see past these twin constraints as they are presently understood and produce something new that paradoxically adheres to the rules of the game and at the same time establishes new rules.[5] This is the meaning of that other famous definition of style, namely Jorge Luis Borges's idea that all great writers create their own precursors.

For Jameson the writer is always both artist and artisan – he or she is a visionary striving after a big idea and someone who works with their hands to painstakingly craft a beautiful object. Speaking of Flaubert's paragraphs, Jameson offers the following telling description: 'Such forms, in which the individual sentences, beaten into solidity, are set together piece by piece into a whole that gives them their meaning, suggest an idea of the work as a craft, like handiwork in silver, an idea which hardly survives at all in the universe of mass merchandise contemporary artists inhabit' (S, 40). The twin pleasures of reading then, which follow from this conception of writing, are both in their own quite different ways anachronistic: the artist's big idea belongs to the future, it is the never realized and perhaps unrealizable utopia of a world differently conceived; while the artisan's handicraft is an echo of an extinct past, a tangible reminder not only of a different way of doing things, but that all things are historical. Consequently, too, the literary text can be treated as an artefact, as a piece of material culture, different only in degree from Mayan urns and Regency vases. Style, if one likes, is the material solution to the abstract problems posed by history understood as the constraints of matter and audience. In this way, all writing offers a certain resistance to the present that Jameson upholds as politically valuable. His twin concerns as cultural critic, voiced insistently throughout his work, namely that historical memory is deteriorating and our sense of the future shrivelling, are obviously of a piece with this view of writing. In his early career, Jameson tended to focus on the craft element, but he would ultimately give much greater weight to the utopian aspect. It is time itself that is the writer's quarry, and, as Jameson insists here, if we focus on narrative exclusively, as is customary in most moral and ethical kinds of literary criticism, which are concerned with 'what happens' and 'what it means for that to happen', then we miss the violence that sentences themselves do to time (*S*, 45).

What style tries to do is create moments – what Deleuze calls (in his book on Proust) 'little pieces of eternity' – that as the simultaneous end and beginning of something are neither swept away with the passing of time nor caught up in the rush of time. In this way thought and expression are fused into one complex structure that requires we look at it from two angles at once, which Jameson would later describe in his book on Adorno as an exercise in 'stereoscopy' (*LM*, 28). 'In philosophy as in literature the distinction between something expressed and the means or form through which it is expressed is archaic: there is no incorrect formulation of a true idea; the search for a proper expression is the same as the search for a wholly adequate notion' (*S*, 67). Style impressed itself upon philosophy as an inescapable – modern – necessity and in the process gave rise to the new thing called theory, which we may henceforth think of as philosophy that has become (extremely!) self-conscious about the effect and condition of writing. This is the situation of the literary critic today, of Jameson himself, and what is clear is that Sartre was one of the first writers to confront it in a clear-sighted way. Style, then, can be viewed as the visible trace of history itself. Sartre's situation was emblematic of much of late-twentieth-century writing. As one of the last modernists Sartre was also a proto-postmodernist inasmuch as his writerly situation anticipates that historical transformation. Jameson describes his situation as follows: 'With the breakdown of traditional life patterns, unquestioned ritual that lives developed along, and with the rise of boredom as a possible quality of life, the notion of an event, of an experience, of something really happening, becomes problematical: when not everything is real living, only certain things can be told and constitute anecdotes or stories' (*S*, 19). The essential coordinates of this situation, particularly the felt unreality of daily life, would intensify in the years to follow, culminating in the appearance of the new situation we know as postmodernism.

Adorno

'The question about poetry after Auschwitz' which tends to preoccupy the majority of Adorno's contemporary readers (many of them under the hallucinogenic influence of Jean-François Lyotard, to be sure, and thus more concerned with showing that his 'totalizing' methodology was somehow totalitarian in spirit if not actuality) as they try to grapple with the changing ethical conditions of our times, is not the essential Adornian question. Now, Jameson says, the crucial question is 'whether you could bear to read Adorno and Horkheimer next to the pool' (*LM*, 248). Such a question, fiercely comical as it is, might go some way to restoring the 'sense of something grim and impending within the polluted sunshine of the shopping mall – some older classical European-style sense of doom and crisis, which even the Common Market countries have cast off in their own chrysalid transmogrification, but which the USA can now use better than they can, being an older and now more ramshackle society by contrast (a little like finally being older than your own father, as Sartre once put it)' (*LM*, 248). Jameson's point is that Adorno's work truly only comes into its own and finds its time, that is, the moment in which its message about the torturous shape of the future coincides with our uncertain sense of the present, a decade or so after his death, in the midst of what Jameson terms full-blown postmodernism.

Written at the close of the 1980s, the decade that saw the triumph of the New Right in the form of a cross-Atlantic hegemony of Reaganism and Thatcherism; the fall of the Berlin Wall and the collapse of 'actually existing socialism'; the crushing defeat of labour and wholesale routing of blue-collar existence as the First World de-industrialized; and, tellingly, the abandoning of Marx as the thinker of collectivity for other contemporary theorists (chiefly Derrida, but also Deleuze, Foucault and Lyotard) apparently favouring the personal, singular and individual; *Late Marxism* is a calculated attempt to produce a portrait of Adorno as the critic we need in such baleful circumstances. 'Here at length, in this decade which has just ended but is still ours, Adorno's prophecies of the "total system" finally came true, in wholly unexpected forms' (*LM*, 5). He was not a thinker of the 1930s, that was Heidegger; nor the 1940s and 1950s, which belonged to Sartre; nor the 1960s, for which we look to Marcuse; and certainly not the 1970s, in which poststructuralism in all its guises triumphed; but, Jameson muses, he might just be the theorist of the 1980s, a long decade whose effects are still being felt. He earns this place in the spotlight because his 'bile is a joyous counter-poison and a corrosive solvent to apply to the surface of "what is" ' (*LM*, 249).

Of course, to say that Adorno is the critic of the 1980s is to challenge the hegemony of the discipline that thinks it somehow defines the period's intellectual sense of itself, namely cultural studies. Any reasonably competent study of the fortunes of academic disciplines and discourses, particularly in the humanities, but by no means confined to that, would have to conclude that in the 1980s cultural studies experienced an incredible rise from basic obscurity at the start of the decade to near hegemony at the end. Jameson's Adorno then is calculated to be a bitter pill rammed down the throat of what he plainly sees as a de-Marxified cultural studies, which in its sometimes facile and frequently ahistorical celebration of 'what is' has tended to shun properly critical negativity in all its forms. I am perhaps over-egging things a bit in putting it this way because Jameson himself is always much more measured than this (but having said that, Eagleton is wrong to say his work lacks polemical fire: the difference – between Eagleton and Jameson, I mean – is that Jameson reserves his rhetorical bullets for the actual enemies of socialist thinking, namely the ideologists and indeed the organs of capitalism).[6]

It is clear though, from his exhaustive review of the mammoth collection of papers edited by Lawrence Grossberg, Cary Nelson and Paula Treichler entitled simply *Cultural Studies*, that cultural studies is the correct recipient (albeit not the only one) of this strong medicine (*OCS*). His chief complaints against cultural studies are that it is situationally unaware and politically misdirected: its approach tends to be narrow and regional in focus and lacking in any sense of the bigger picture, of the totality, or what in an older Marxist language would be known as the base; by the same token, and for essentially the same reasons, it pursues a line of inquiry that concentrates on the peculiar and the different, and not the strategic alliance or common cause. In return cultural studies has two main complaints about Jameson's work: the first manifests itself as a low-level grumbling about his gloominess, read off his supposed failure to perceive the dissident and resistive pleasures being had by people all around him; and the second, much more problematically, manifests itself as a high-minded gripe against his 'elitist' totalizations, which are problematic either because they are too inclusive or not inclusive enough.[7] Altogether, these complaints, both those Jameson himself makes and the ones directed against him, turn on two concepts that are effectively the twin axes, the north and south poles if you will, of *Late Marxism*, namely 'nominalization' and 'totalization'.

Readers of *Postmodernism, or, the Cultural Logic of Late Capitalism*, will have noticed that these two terms – 'nominalization' and 'totalization' – are central to that work as well. Provided it is understood that *Late Marxism* has its own job of work to do, it is productive to read these two books as companion volumes, each somehow extending and completing the other, the one outlining the architecture and origin of these concepts and the other demonstrating their utility through a variety of critical applications. Indeed, in the closing pages of *Late Marxism*, Jameson will go so far as to say that postmodernism is a form – or, rather, a consequence and culmination – of nominalism or its structural-other positivism inasmuch as it 'wants to reduce us to the empirical present (or to use the empirical present as the sole pattern for imagining other situations and other temporal moments)' (*LM*, 249).[8] Nominalism simultaneously describes a late-modern or proto-postmodern philosophical tendency, which finds its keenest expression in aesthetics as a refusal of the universal, but is in reality a much larger problem than that (as Jameson cautions, confining discussions of Adorno's work to the realm of the aesthetics is one of the strategies that have been deployed to contain the more difficult political questions his work poses, beyond the fate of art as such), and an historical event (*LM*, 157). Nominalism is not a style, then, but a condition, or better a historical situation, brought about by the progressive deterioration of the 'transcendent' in all forms of thinking. It implies a 'commitment to empirical facts and worldly phenomena in which the abstract – interpretation fully as much as general ideas, larger synchronic collective units fully as much as dia-chronic narratives or genealogies – is increasingly constricted, when not systematically pursued and extirpated as a relic and a survival of older traditional, "metaphysical", or simply old-fashioned and antiquated thoughts and categories' (*LM*, 89). As Jameson shows elsewhere, the pedantry of deconstruction, the ruthless way it roots out 'undecidables', and uncovers all kinds of traces, spoors, cracks, fissures and erasures, is of a piece with the positivism Adorno saw philosophy descending into (*PCL*, 250). Under such conditions, the notion of totality, which is effectively the supreme form of abstraction available, should be seen as a solution – its needfulness may perhaps be read off the level and intensity of critical ire it excites.

Jameson could not be less unequivocal in his judgement of the importance of totalization: Adorno's 'life work stands or falls with the concept of "totality" ' (*LM*, 9). But as I have already suggested, the same can be said of Jameson's own work. More ink has been spilled denouncing both Adorno's and Jameson's use of 'totalization' than any other concept in their respective critical arsenals. We can simply say that no other concept typically associated with their work has been so drastically and well-nigh universally misunderstood. Jameson himself diagnoses the various attacks on his use of a 'totalizing' method as symptomatic of a deep-seated antipathy toward utopian thinking, 'such that a Utopian and revolutionary politics, correctly associated with total-isation and a certain "concept" of totality, is to be eschewed because it leads fatally to Terror: a notion at least as old as Edmund Burke, but helpfully revived, after innumerable restatements during the Stalin period, by the Cambodian atrocities' (*PCL*, 401). Critics of this notion have (rather childishly, it must be said) tended to equate an attempt to try to generate an abstraction – that is, a concept – able to account for the global situation today with the desire to somehow control the world or survey it. It is as childish and stupid as, say, treating as equivalent physicist Stephen Hawkings's desire for a theory of everything with colonialist Cecil Rhodes's infamous desire to colonize all the planets in the solar system. In philosophical terms the confusion of Adorno's 'totality' with the nightmarish 'total systems' of Weber and Foucault is a category mistake. Totality on both Adorno's and Jameson's usage would always include (in some properly antagonistic schematization) those strategies and tactics of 'resistance' which appear forcibly excluded from Weber's and Foucault's systems, but not out of some feeble faith in the power of alternative identities, or some such phantasm (itself yet another variant on the delusion of the omnipotence of thought), but because the concept itself is bigger than, or rather implies an entity greater than, any human system could possibly be. The proper spatial and temporal dimensions of the concept of totality are the universe and the infinite process of evolution. Darwin rather than Marx, or rather Marx by way of Darwin, is the correct theoretical progenitor of the term; as such, it should be treated as a 'scientific' (in Marx's sense) rather than an 'ideological' concept, the implication being that it is an inhuman concept in the best (i.e. Marxist) sense of the word.

> Marx's own relationship to Darwin is well known; the abortive dedication of *Capital* Volume 1 (1867) to the author of *The Origin of Species* (1857) was a little more than a salute from one initiator of a Copernican revolution to another. It was meant to affirm the subsumption of human history – for the first time scientifically disengaged by historical materialism – under natural history – something henceforth indissociable from Darwin's own work and theorisation. (*LM*, 94–95)

Totalization, then, at its most abstract, is a species perspective on history, but we should take care here not to turn this into something it is not, namely an ahistorical exercise in sociobiology (á la Robert Ardrey, Konrad Lorenz or Jared Diamond) or that new thing arisen out of Deleuze studies which we might call sociophysics (á la Delanda, Massumi, Protevi). It is not, in other words, an attempt to find some kind of 'spiritual automaton' within humans (human nature, instincts, drives, neurobiology, etc.) that can account for their behaviour, particularly those violent and destructive actions we want most to disown at the species level, in a way that makes it seem 'natural'. That is to say, any treatment of nature as some absolute first term is decidedly not what Adorno had in mind since, as Jameson points out, 'the peculiar originality of Adorno's and Horkheimer's conception of a "dialectic of enlightenment" is that it excludes any beginning or first term' (*LM*, 100). Nature no more explains history than history explains nature, but read together nature and history bring about a mutual estrangement – a negative dialectic – of the respective presuppositions that have built up around these two processes. This amounts to saying that there is no human action that can be treated as straightforwardly 'natural' or 'historical': a proposition that becomes particularly illuminating when we focus on long-held assumptions about humankind's supposed destructiveness. The effect of this is to compel us to 'think another side, an outside, an external face of the concept which, like that of the moon, can never be directly visible or accessible to us: but we must vigilantly remember and reckon that other face into our sense of the concept while remaining within it in the old way and continuing to use and think it' (*LM*, 25). In other words, we can neither rely on nature or history to provide us with our starting points or answers in the last instance, nor jettison them completely in favour of some other new terms which could, since obviously enough that would simply duplicate the already rebuked structure of thought. Substituting 'genetics' or 'endocrinology' or some such other microcosmic inquiry for nature is no solution to the problem described above of creating phantasmatic 'spiritual automatons' to explain human behaviour in either or both the first and last instance. What should be clear then is that totality is effectively a codeword for that other famous Adornian notion, 'negative dialectics'.

As the history of 'race' reveals readily enough, we use nature to conceal history, even from ourselves – thus slavery was justified on the grounds that 'black' people were inferior, inhuman, without souls and so on; yet, by the same token, it is precisely nature, the fact that black people are people just like us, that brings about the needed deconcealment – the more science tried to show 'they' were different, the more it ended up showing 'they' were the same, forcing the acknowledgement that slavery is historical. But if this extinguishes the idea that slavery cannot be justified on the grounds of racial superiority, it does not similarly extinguish the idea that nature cannot still be blamed somehow. For what rises like a phoenix from the ashes of racial superiority is the idea of human nature itself, which is supposedly shot-through with all kinds of unsavoury tendencies to act violently toward fellow humans.

Instead of slavery justified on the spurious grounds of racial superiority we get slavery justified on the unassailably scientific grounds of human viciousness – the instincts, the genes, the chromosomes, something in us beyond our control is ultimately to blame. We enslave because we are fundamentally mean, ruthless creatures, constantly striving to improve our lot at whatever cost to others. By this means, science becomes the alibi of ahistorical thought, it simultaneously excuses the subject from having to take responsibility for his or her actions (it couldn't be helped, it was in their nature), and reifies their solar position as the central agents of history by making individual desires the motive force of all change.

History only gets us part of the way out of this dilemma because even if it can show that the science is false, or – what amounts to the same thing – used to self-serving ends, it cannot account fully for the logical next question of why we should want to so deceive ourselves in the first place. If we could show that there is no such thing as a destructive urge in humans and that all the science supporting its existence was bogus, or skewed to highlight destructiveness and downplay more salutary urges, such as those which tend toward nurturing and caring, then we would still want to know why we find it so satisfying to think of ourselves as destructive. I hasten to add that those views of human nature which regard it as primarily nurturing and caring are no less problematic. In other words, we are constantly looking to the body, as nature incarnate, to bring history (as the remorseless questioning of what is) to an end, only to find it recommence before our eyes in its new guise as science. This gives rise to a uniquely Adornian problem that Jameson has effectively made his own:

> This is to say purity in philosophical thinking or writing . . . the unmixed or 'intrinsic', is as impossible as it is undesirable: something that holds for the individual concept as well and also – paradoxically for those who think of Adorno as in this area the very quintessence of the aesthete – for the work of art. What the concept cannot say must somehow, by its imperfection, be registered within it . . . Those for whom dialectical thought in general, and Adorno's writing in particular, are uncongenial have seen this impurity at work more vividly than the sympathisers. (*LM*, 30)

There is no clearer explanation and defence of the dialectical sentence than this – if it is tortured and torturing, then it must be so because it has such a job of contradictory work to do. It must simultaneously produce a study of a textual object and the 'concepts and categories (themselves historical) that we necessarily bring to the object' (*PU*, 109).

Brecht

Jameson's book on Brecht is probably his most forthright demonstration of the dictum that all histories are histories of the present, a dictum that knows its own pungent Brechtian inflection: 'Don't start from the good old things, but rather the bad new ones.'[9] Jameson's gambit is to concentrate on what he calls Brecht's usefulness, rather than either his posterity, greatness or canonicity, as a way of demonstrating not only the continuing relevance of his thought, but more particularly its undiminished capacity to surprise and instruct. Jameson presents us with an always untimely (in Nietzsche's sense) and resolutely modern Brecht whose work is defined by its discontinuity and fragmentation, but nevertheless knows a certain 'unity in dispersal' (*BM*, 6). Because Brecht's gift to us is a method not a philosophical system, we receive it – after the fashion of the Chinese proverb Jameson cites in *The Political Unconscious* – as an axe with which to make another axe (*PU*, 13). If Jameson is forced to acknowledge that to many Brecht is dead, a spent force in literature and criticism, it is only so he can exact the exquisite revenge of unveiling an undead Brecht whose spectre haunts not only Europe but the fully-globalized world. Jameson's book on Brecht is written with the same combative and polemical spirit as Terry Eagleton's comparable study of Walter Benjamin, written 'to get at him before the opposition does'.[10] By setting aside such false problems as whether or not Brecht was foremost a poet or playwright, or whether his theory somehow transcended mere dramaturgy, as well as several decades of critical pigeon-holing of him as 'anti-naturalist', *Brecht and Method* 'blasts free' a revolutionary Brecht by showing that such metaphors as 'blasting free' (Benjamin's famous phrase, which Eagleton makes the centrepiece of his book) are Brechtian in the first place (*BM*, 3).[11] Jameson's Brecht emerges as one of the great, if not always properly acknowledged, inspirations of twentieth-century theory (*BM*, 11). The larger goal of *Brecht and Method*, however, is to rescue the idea that art can be pedagogical, an idea that in full-blown postmodernism is more surely dead and buried than Brecht.

If Brecht is dead to us today, it is because we have Brecht fatigue – his literary star once shone so bright it seared our eyes and left us unable to see where Brecht might be able to take us in the future. Brecht's work was perfectly suited to the contradictory demands of the 1960s and

1970s, the peak decades of his posthumous fame.[12] As Jameson puts it, for 'bourgeois publics, fasting on a diet of theatrical minimalism' there was Brecht's operatic lavishness of set and costume as well as the richness of his textuality – encompassing, as it did, everything from traditional Noh drama, to Chinese mask plays and Chicago gangsters; for the left, 'a whole theory and strategy and political writing was set in place which could be transferred to other media and situations' (as exemplified by the allegedly Brechtian films of Jean-Luc Godard and Alexander Kluge, as well as the installations of Hans Haacke and Joseph Beuys), because it carved out a space for avant-garde art as always already political – it was in this sense a sometimes too comfortable alibi for artistic experimentation, giving us a watered-down gesture where a more robust *gestus* was needed; while for the Third World, Brecht's interest in a kind of peasant theatre 'made plenty of room for Chaplinesque buffoonery, mime, dance, and all kinds of pre-realistic, pre-bourgeois stagecraft and performance' and 'secured for Brecht the historical position of a catalyst and an enabling model in the emergence of many "non-Western" theatres from Brazil to Turkey, from the Philippines to Africa' (*BM*, 18). In so doing, Brecht's work simultaneously fulfilled three different kinds of needs – he was a brilliant innovator and his work sparked ideas in other great innovators in an age avid for such innovation (this period was literally the great age of theatrical experimentation – Peter Brook, Jerzy Grotowski and Richard Schechner were all at the peak of their powers); it created a new way of making political art, one that, crucially, after the dreary years of 'approved' Zhadanovite forms, was exciting and complex; and, in bringing these two factors together, gave the Third World, and indeed all forms of minor politics, a new kind of theatrical voice, which was at once strident and moralizing and anti-authoritarian and amoral. Bequeathed this clichéd image of a Brecht of the 1960s and 1970s struggling for relevance in the new millennium, Jameson's task is clear – he must bring forward a Brecht fit for the jaded and cynical era we know as postmodernism, without at the same time constructing an artificial or postmodern Brecht.[13] This Brecht will be enabling and in Deleuze's sense joyous (*BM*, 29).

What does this Brecht look like? Crystalline, pyramidal, multi-layered, monadic are all words Jameson uses to describe this Brecht whose art is, he suggests, best understood in terms of autonomization. The term derives from a remark by the great German modernist writer, Alexander Döblin, Brecht cited as a watchword: 'Unlike the dramatic, the narrative you can cut up into so many separate pieces as though with scissors' (*BM*, 43). Godard's quip, that a story must have a beginning, a middle and end, but not necessarily in that order, is obviously of a piece with this line of thinking. Our first glimpse of what autonomization looks like on stage is to be found in so-called Brechtian technique, emblematized in his theory that the audience should be able to watch theatre in the same detached manner as they would a boxing match. Rather than strive for empathy (*Einfühlung*), the standard goal of naturalistic theatre (whose essential features live on in Hollywood cinema), Brecht sought analytic judgement, the coolness of calculation not the warmth of feeling, which some have read as anti-identification.[14] He wanted the audience to see that it is the protagonists' situation which determines the action, not their characters, this being the essential difference between his epic theatre and the more familiar tragic theatre. Thus, Brecht's *Hamlet* does not attribute his 'famous hesitations ("sicklied o'er with the pale cast of thought", etc.)' to 'some heightened, "modern", individual-istic psychology or subjectivity emerging from the formulaic Middle Ages but, rather, the other way round: to the interference of these two cultural patterns, themselves the force fields of two distinct modes of production' (*BM*, 106). To achieve this 'estrangement effect' (*Verfremdung-seffekt*), as it will be called, Brecht utilized a wide range of de-naturalizing strategies, most of which have now been naturalized all over again as the standard repertoire of 'tricks' available to any good *metteur en scène*. Among the more famous is his use of captions or intertitles dropped down from the ceiling to name a song or frame an action, which are calculated to break not only the flow of the action on stage, but also the logic of narrative itself by telling the audience ahead of time how things will turn out (like the character who says 'I'm just off to the thirty years war'). Instead of the affecting suspense of an unfolding story or drama of a life, the audience is given the bracing jolt – i.e., the lesson – of life as it is viewed and judged by history books.

But Jameson is also anxious that autonomization be seen as a larger issue than mere theatrical technique and directs our attention to its social and philosophical dimensions. Here we must connect autonomi-zation to Niklas Luhmann's concept of differentiation, which describes a similar process in the social realm itself (*SM*, 90). For Jameson, then, autonomization is an ambivalent process – it owes a great deal of its psychic energy to the less than salutary processes of social autonomiza-tion, such as the various dismantlings of life–world connections that in Marxist discourse are known as alienation, but at the same time artistic autonomization serves to transform that social disconnection Luhmann called 'differentiation' into an opportunity for a new collective form of thinking to come into being. Reflecting this ambivalence, modernist autonomization has two contradictory impulses – one in the direction of a kind of aesthetic minimalism, namely towards the smallest significant unit, to the point even – *pace* John Cage – of upholding silence itself; the other in the direction of mega-structures, gigantic uncontainable, perhaps even unfinishable works like Musil's *Man Without Qualities* that display no particular need for closure (thus paradoxically Proust's *Remembrance of Things Past* although twice the length of Musil's unfinished masterpiece is nevertheless an example of the former trend toward minimalism: it is true it is not minimalist in Beckett's sparse sense, but it is probably more concerned with the smallest unit of significance than any other text – certainly no other text has ever attended at such length to the smallest gestures of daily life). 'Both tendencies are present in Brecht', Jameson writes, 'along with a good deal of incompleteness as well' (*BM*, 45). But the crucial point here is that reification, which is at once the means and object (not end) of autonomization, both what enables it and what it is against, is a 'tendential social law'. Here we are returned once more to Adorno, who, as Jameson points out, 'is only the foremost' among those who explained modernism in terms of reification in this twofold way.[15] Brecht's uptake of this 'method' 'incorporates the spirit of the Leninist admiration for Fordism' and at the same time seeks to make it comprehensible in human terms by rendering it absurd. Cynicism is, in this sense, the only sensible or indeed intelligible response to capitalism.

> The process of aesthetic autonomisation, breaking the action up into its smallest parts, thus has symbolic as well as epistemological meaning: it shows what the act 'really' is, no doubt, but the very activity of breaking it up and 'analysing' it is itself a joyous process, a kind of creative play, in which new acts are formed together out of pieces in the old, in which the reified surface of a period seemingly beyond history and beyond change now submits to a first ludic un-building, before arriving at a real social and revolutionary collective reconstruction. (*BM*, 47)

'One hesitates' to call this 'either an ethical or a psychological or psychoanalytic re-enactment', Jameson continues, although patently it shares a family resemblance with those things, because it is not strictly speaking a personal matter (*BM*, 47). Rather it uses the individual case in order to make a general point about the possibility of individual action in a global situation which seems immune to change.[16] This is, finally, how we should understand that most famous of Brechtian categories: the estrangement effect. 'Brecht offered many "definitions" of this term, which seems to have migrated from the *"ostranenie"* or "making-strange" of the Russian Formalists via any number of visits to Berlin by Soviet Modernists like Eisenstein or Tretiakov. Like Eisenstein's concept of "montage" [and Jameson's own concept of "metacommentary"], it permitted him to organise and coordinate a great many distinctive features of his theatrical practice and aesthetic.'[17] At bottom, though, it must do two things: it must jolt us out of the waking slumber of daily life and it must cause us to think about what it was that jolted us; but it also has to prevent us from sliding back into that slumber. Thus the most adequate definition of the estrangement effect is going to be that which calls for yet another estrangement effect in its own right. This is illustrated in Brecht's discussion on the usability of the dramatization of a traffic accident for this purpose – if done realistically enough, it would certainly jolt the audience out of its slumber, but would it make them think? It might make them think about the cause of the accident, or even less interestingly the apportioning of blame, but it would not necessarily make them think about what it means to think about a traffic accident. So the true estrangement effect comes into effect when a means is found to compel the audience into this state of self-reflexivity whereby they think about what it means to think. Here the use of a caption informing the audience ahead of time what is going to happen might be what is needed to stop the action being perceived as something calling for pathos and see it instead as a 'lesson'.[18] The more general lesson is that violence alone is not sufficient to engender thought – what one needs, rather, is the violence of thought itself. This is what is meant by the received definition of the estrangement effect as the alteration of our perception such that what appeared natural is revealed as historical after all (*PH*, 58).

Jameson's Brecht teaches us how to act. His art is mindful of the 'dirty pleasures' and the unsubtle addictiveness of capitalism; it knows how difficult it can be to persuade oneself that there is something better to be had, and yet through absurdity, humour, contradiction and paradox rouses within us the strength and energy needed to slough off the velvet-lined shackles of commodity fetishism. But, as Jameson reminds us, if 'the Brechtian doctrine of activity' was 'energizing' to a whole generation of artists, activists and scholars – the generation for whom Brecht was a contemporary, or near-contemporary – it was 'because activity and praxis were on the agenda', whereas today that is no longer the case. In fact, the very opposite seems to be the case. 'Stasis today, all over the world – in the twin condition of the market and globalisation, commodification and financial speculation – does not even take on the baleful religious sense of an implacable Nature; but it certainly seems to have outstripped any place for human agency, and to have rendered the latter obsolete' (*BM*, 4). In contemporary social and political theory this immobilization, by which Jameson means political inactivity, indeed political inanition, has been theorized or accounted for in two main ways: first of all, under the rubric of 'Risk Society', the German sociologist Ulrich Beck has built an entire sub-branch of sociology around the observation that the majority of decisions which by rights belong to the realm of the political are no longer made there, but have been inexorably driven into the sub-political realms of the market and the bureaucracy (he means, for instance, the decision to stop producing vinyl records in favour of CDs, which without our consent or desire renders obsolescent our entire record collection, compelling us to re-buy it all in the new format); second of all, under the rubric of 'cynical reason', the German cultural critic Peter Sloterdijk has given us a way of describing how we continue to function under such potentially demoralizing conditions (we know things are bad, but since we cannot do anything about it why worry?)[19] Most of us have come to these concepts via Slavoj Žižek's Lacanian refunctioning (*umfunktionieren*) of them, to return us once more to Brecht, which attempts to restore what is missing from both, namely the possibility of action. Žižek's turn to the figures of Christ, Lenin and St Paul is precisely directed at developing both a philosophy and an ideology of action.[20] But, insofar as these concepts are estranging in this sense of rendering historical what previously appeared natural, they are already enabling of action, for that which is historical is the product of human labour and is therefore susceptible to further change via the same means.

The usefulness of Brecht reveals itself in the end to be precisely the resurrection of the idea that critical work can be useful, that it can achieve change, and that the effort to think new thoughts, to create new ideas, is not useless. And as we confront a new century presenting us with innumerable apparently insurmountable problems ranging from the AIDS epidemic in Africa, the worldwide threat of 'bird flu', to global warming and the unilateralist aggression of the lone superpower, we have never needed to hear this message more. At a more local level, Brecht is additionally useful because his work – read against the grain, particularly by people like Roland Barthes – is the source of some of the astringent anti-dialectical positions (*PD*, 369).

Barthes

No 'satisfactory study of the career of Roland Barthes can afford to omit his Brechtian (as well as his Sartrean) origins: his classic *Mythologies* paved the way for the triumphant entry of the estrangement-effect into French theory' (*BM*, 38). It is Barthes's honour, as it were, to have been the first to create a truly usable form of Brecht's method: 'Barthes's was a textbook "application" of the method to a range of social and cultural phenomena, along with a theorisation of the objects of estrangement in proto-linguistic terms, which had its own generative influence on the linguistics-based evolution of so-called structuralism itself. (The other dimension of Barthes's early work – which retains its immense historical significance – his own work on literary history, as that found lapidary expression in *Writing Degree Zero*, is rather of Sartrean origin)' (*BM*, 173). Thus Jameson's book on Brecht, discussed above, has as an additional reward, a kind of bonus pleasure if you will, of giving us a remarkably new or rather newly estranged Barthes. It proposes that Barthes's *Mythologies* gave rise to theory not as many have argued because it introduced a whole generation of students and scholars to semiotics, but because it provided a vivid example of the application of the Brechtian principle of the estrangement effect in academic writing. What looked like an exciting new theory of language was in fact the estrangement effect at work: to insist that a word or image is first of all a sign is to break the naturalistic assumption of how its meaning is conveyed. For Jameson there are essentially two Roland Barthes – there is Roland Barthes the sociologist, the author of *Mythologies*, *The Fashion System* and *Empire of Signs*, and there is Roland Barthes the literary critic, author of *Writing Degree Zero* and *S/Z* – the first is Brechtian and the latter Sartrean (*PH*, 146). It was Barthes's ability to synthesize these two traditions and then in his fashion transcend them that accords him a special place in Jameson's selection of desert-island theory books. However, there also exists a third Roland Barthes, the anti-Left Roland Barthes of *The Pleasure of the Text*, which gives us cause to wonder whether Barthes should not finally be excluded from the list of formative influences.[21]

Exorcising this third Barthes is, I want to suggest, the point of Jameson's foregrounding of Barthes's Brecthian and Sartrean origins. It redeems for the contemporary Left an important thinker whose work owes such an obvious debt to Left philosophical traditions. Let us start then with the infamous Barthes whose 'oddly defensive' book, *The Pleasure of the Text*, is for Jameson such an important artefact of the backlash against the Left (*BM*, 65). If *Mythologies* was the inaugural text of theory, then *The Pleasure of the Text* was the book that set theory on its course for its own 'crisis', namely that crisis the 'What's Left of Theory?' conference in Hobart in 2001 tried to articulate by compressing two questions into one: If theory is an essentially Left invention, as Jameson himself has argued it is, then can we still call a theory that repudiates the Left 'theory'? Not all theory does repudiate the Left, of course, but it is certainly the case that significant sections do, especially the deconstructionist chapter which espouses the view that everything is political, but only at the price of there being no acceptable form of party politics, no form of actual political practice that does not compromise its rarefied vision of 'the political' as an impossible ideal. Jameson's enthusiasm for Derrida's *Spectres of Marx*, which his sterner colleagues on the Left could never be persuaded to share, followed precisely this logic: he saw that Derrida's gesture of speaking about Marx directly would have the effect of compelling deconstruction to confront a specifically Left conception of the political, and that could only be a good thing (*MPL*). The deeper issue here is whether or not we should or can be pluralist about theory? This brings us to the second question. If the discourse we used to know as theory has been depoliticized in such a way that none of its original Left impulses remain intact or active, then what is the new thing that the Left is producing today? If theory has been so thoroughly compromised by the doctrine of optionality, then what is the new thing thinkers on the Left cannot not choose? Jameson's answer would seem to be: if a little bit of *The Pleasure of the Text* takes us away from a Left politics, then a lot of *Mythologies* and *Writing Degree Zero* can bring us back. Such, I believe is Jameson's gambit – his work on Barthes can thus be read as a cautionary tale warning us against the temptations of individualizing politics.

The strong form of this object lesson will be presented in *The Seeds of Time* in the form of an argument against a politics of difference, on the understanding that 'group politics only begin to evolve in a radical direction when the various groups [groups that today identify themselves under the banners of categories like race, gender, sexuality] all arrive at the common problem and necessity of their strategic interrelationships, something for which any number of historic terms are available from Gramsci's "historic bloc" through alliance politics to the "popular front" of "marginalities" currently proposed by "queer theory" ' (*ST*, 64–65). Jameson adds that it is only in view of some grim caricature of Stalinism that such a collectivizing of revolutionary energies could amount to their negation or repression, and it is to be hoped that we are beyond thinking such things. Just such a caricature, however, appears to have shaped Barthes's thinking about Left politics, at least in his later years when he wrote *The Pleasure of the Text*. For a great many French intellectuals in this period, Stalinism not only represented all that was wrong about Left politics, but seemed to define it *tout court*. Marxism equalled Stalinism. Once this viewpoint became entrenched, however blunted and lacking nuance it is, it became difficult for even the most committed and engaged Marxists to maintain their commitment – Sartre's famous response was to say that if he could not be pro-communism (in its Stalinist mode), then neither could he be anti-communist since that would be a betrayal of everything he believed in, so rather than that he would be anti-anti-communist.[22] Not all intellectuals were capable of this brave dialectical stance. However, it was the Left's doctrinal belief in the so-called 'stages' theory of history, for which 'Hegelianism' is frequently blamed, that French intellectuals detested most, and this more than anything else turned them away from Left politics.[23] The 'stages' theory of history is the 'vulgar Marxist' view that historical change can only occur when certain predetermined cultural and economic milestones are reached (thus before Mao and Lenin it was said peasants could not lead a communist revolution because they were not yet properly plebianized). According to this doctrine there is a right time for a revolution, but as that time never seems to arrive the Party apparatus spends most of its time counselling – indeed, forcibly restraining – its membership to be patient. Impatient for change, temperamentally disinclined to embrace any doctrine unquestioningly, much less one with such a repugnant recent history of brutality, and in the absence of alternative models of actually existing socialism, once staunchly Left critics like Barthes (but one could also mention Deleuze, Foucault and Lyotard) started a backlash against it by advocating a free-spirited anarchism.

The trajectory of Barthes's drift away from any politics – not just Left politics – can be seen quite clearly in the following sentence from *The Pleasure of the Text* which may be taken as emblematic: 'The pleasure of the text is that moment when my body pursues its own ideas – for my body does not have the same ideas I do.'[24] The body as site of pleasure, restless in its pursuit of its own kind of satisfaction, and heedless of the mind's needs, would henceforth be the site of anti-politics. Like the cartoon philistine in a contemporary art gallery who says, 'I don't know much about art, but I know what I like', this body knows what its likes and needs and wants are, and cares for nothing else. It does not want to know about art, it wants only to selfishly catalogue its sources of pleasure and extol these in quasi-religious terms – its pleasures are always at once epiphanies, inklings of some godly other, and little deaths, earthly mortification at its most sublime. This body regards all politics, but particularly that branch of it Foucault would later call 'governmental-ity', namely the bureaucratization of daily life, now routinely referred to by another of Foucault's neologisms 'biopower', as an intolerable oppression. It will not wait in line nor suffer to be told what it can and cannot do – everything is art to this body which knows what it likes and trusts only its own viscera. Art to this body must be affecting, it must move the blood and stir the soul, but it need not make us think (on this last point Deleuze differs quite dramatically, only that which makes us think qualifies as art for Deleuze). Jameson reads Barthes's break as being at once in step with history, inasmuch as it occurs at a moment he identifies as the onset of postmodernism, and, as it were, out of step with history, because it turns away from political questions at a moment when such considerations were at the forefront of daily life. 'The very date of that influential, fragmentary statement – 1973 – is in retrospect charged with significance. Making a break dramatized by the emer-gence of the oil weapon and the onset of a global economic crisis that is still with us (and expressed politically in such different events as the Chilean Coup and in France the "common program" of the Left), the general moment from 1972 to 1974 can be seen as the definitive end of whatever, worldwide, came to be known as the 60s' (*IT2*, 65). In a moment of profound historical crisis when neither reformism nor totali-tarianism, democracy nor republicanism, seem to offer any way out of the impasse Barthes retreats into the knowing-body.

But even as Barthes himself moved away from politics, his work com-pelled those who remained behind to confront such questions as he raised in political terms. Thus without necessarily wanting to, Barthes helped to inaugurate a kind of politics of pleasure that had a particular resonance for feminism, although it took a rather divided stand on the subject: on the one hand, thinkers like Germaine Greer upheld the radical right to equal pleasure for women, while thinkers like Laura Mulvey showed that pleasure, particularly the scopic or visual kind, is in its own way a repressing political force. If one defines the gaze as the pleasure of looking at another, then how is one to escape it? Greer's late work on the pleasure of looking at boys would seem to be an attempt to square the circle and, as it were, balance the ledger, but it is trapped within the very logic it seeks to subvert. You cannot undo the power behind the gaze, or indeed the power of the gaze, by widening the angle of viewing to include those who had previously escaped its attention. If we substitute the more overtly political term (taken from Foucault) surveillance for look or gaze, then it becomes rather obvious just how flawed this logic is: extending the gaze to include boys simply enhances the efficacy of the gaze.

The feminist response to this problematic adumbrates a more basic problem or question facing all critical thinkers and writers. Is dissent a matter of production or reception? Dissent is obviously a loaded term, but we can rewrite it as difference, provided it is understood that by 'difference' one means a determinate break with the continuum of the present. In this respect one can further rewrite the problem in terms of a choice between modernism's passionate *cri du coeur* 'make it new' and postmodernism's dispassionate plea that 'there are no right or wrong readings, only stronger or weaker misreadings'. This in itself already knows the great antecedent of Edmund Burke's distinction between the Beautiful and the Sublime, except there as Jameson points out the body expresses itself through fear not pleasure (*IT2*, 73). Barthes had a bet each way – in *Writing Degree Zero* he took modernism to its logical extreme by arguing for a 'white' or 'bleached' writing that was so new as to be without precedent and therefore in a quite deliberate sense unreadable and more importantly unredeemable by either the Left or the Right; while in *The Pleasure of the Text* he abandons the gesture of writing altogether and gives priority to reading, which in his hands becomes – ironically enough – the new writing. His aesthetic judgement favours that writing which induces the reader to want to emulate it, to write not read the text (*IT1*, 21). As a reader he is a writer.

> But one cannot conclude all this without some final evaluation of Barthes himself, so ambiguous a figure. Is it necessary to recall that the early Barthes *was* political, and that he furnished (and books like *Mythologies* continue to furnish) us with critical instruments and weapons of an overt political capability? (*IT2*, 69)

This is the Barthes of the Brecht book, the Barthes Jameson is, as it were, trying to rescue if not redeem. In the end, Jameson offers two kinds of summary judgements on Barthes's career, both of which chime well with his analysis of Brecht, but tell us something of his own concerns as well. The first, as we have seen, is that Barthes created politically enabling critical tools – even at his most apolitical or anti-political, when his thought turned exclusively to the solipsistic pleasures and displeasures of the body, particularly his own body, he nonetheless estranged that body and taught us to think with the body and in the process politicized not only the body but its affects: boredom, pleasure, ecstasy and so on.

The second is that it is more productive to read Barthes as a practitioner than a theorist – his work offers textbook examples of how to refunction 'Bachelardian phenomenology (in his book on Michelet), Sartrean Marxism (in *Writing Degree Zero*), Hjelmslevian linguistics, but also Brechtean *Verfremdung* (in *Mythologies*), orthodox Freudianism (in *On Racine*), hard-core semiotics (in *Système de la mode*), *Tel Quel* textual productivity, as well as Lacanian psychoanalysis (in *S/Z* itself), poststructuralism (in *Le Plaisir du texte*)' (*IT1*, 21). What his work shows then is what each of these theories can do, what their limits and shortcomings are, as well as their lines of flight, the creative trajectories one can take with them. His work is saved from a descent into an unappealing smorgasbord of theoretical options by the rancorous way he sets aside his own experiments as peculiar failures that might be redeemed if only a new theory is now applied. It will not be a mistake to say that these are values Jameson prioritizes in his own work. He is at once a relentless inventor of concepts and a voracious *refunctioner* of concepts.

Notes

1 Unfortunately the full text remains unpublished, although there is a fragment available in the forum on the future of theory hosted by *Critical Inquiry*. See *STS*.

2 The most succinct expression of Jameson's view of the historical origins of theory is his essay 'Periodizing the 60s', which was originally written as a kind of prologue to a never completed cultural history of the 1960s. It has subsequently been refunctioned as a pendant essay to the programme piece on postmodernism. See *IT1*, 186–87; but see also *WS*, 19 and *PCL*, 397. His disputation of the notion that reading is a kind of writing is found in *MF*, 415.

3 As Mike Davis's (2003) history of San Diego illustrates, San Diego was a nexus point for both these currents: as a major naval base and military research and development city the war was visible there in a way that it would not have been in Boston or Connecticut had Jameson stayed on the east coast; by the same token as a new university that purposely sought to explore alternative paradigms of thought UCSD was the site of profound counter-cultural expressions.

4 I argue this more fully in I. Buchanan, 'Reading Jameson Dogmatically', *Historical Materialism* 10:3 (2002) pp. 223–43.

5 This is essentially Bourdieu's argument too. See for instance P. Bourdieu, *The Field of Cultural Production: Essays on Art and Literature* (Cambridge: Polity Press, 1993).

6 T. Eagleton, 'Making a Break', *London Review of Books*, 28:5 (2006) p. 26.

7 I develop this point in more detail in Buchanan,'Reading Jameson Dogmatically'. But see I. Buchanan, *Deleuzism: A Metacommentary* (Edinburgh: Edinburgh University Press, 2000) pp. 143–74 for an account of the productive connections that can be made between Jameson and Deleuze.

8 Jameson's critique of 'New Historicism' (*PCL*, 190–93) is staged in precisely these terms.

9 Jameson (*CT*, 93–94) commends this dictum as a strategy for engaging postmodernism.

10 T. Eagleton, *Walter Benjamin, or Towards a Revolutionary Criticism* (London: Verso, 1981) p. xii.

11 On this score, too, we may wonder at the influence of Brecht on Eagleton, for after all, as he informs us in the introduction to his Benjamin book, he wrote it on the back of his 1979 play *Brecht and Company*.

12 In Jameson's (*CT*, 74) view, this was an age in which the most significant creative figures in theatre were *metteurs en scène* rather than playwrights.

13 For Jameson, antiquarianism (reviving the past) and anachronism (the re-writing of past texts in the image of the present) are the twin dangers of all cultural history. See *PU*, 17–18; *IT2*, 17–71.

14 On this particular point, Jameson observes: 'I think that Brecht's positions are better read not as a refusal of identification but, rather, as the consequences to be drawn from the fact that such a thing never existed in the first place' (*BM*, 53).

15 Reification 'defines the situation and the element which the work wishes to resist, but also defines the logic of that resistance, as a kind of homeopathic remedy which fights a general logic of objectification by way of the objectification of its own forms' (*BM*, 46).

16 I will take the liberty here of suggesting that Deleuze's notion of 'counter-actualization' describes precisely this process for which Jameson seems to lack an appropriate term. See G. Deleuze, *The Logic of Sense* (trans. M. Lester with C. Stivale; London: Athlone Press, 1990) p. 150; Buchanan, *Deleuzism*, pp. 77–87. This may well be the path the Deleuzian friends of Brecht take in order to show that what Brecht called contradiction was 'only a larger tent or umbrella for rich and subtle differentiations of all kinds' (*BM*, 79).

17 *BM*, 39.

18 In Australia in the late 1990s, public health officials discovered to their utter dismay that the grisly advertisements they had commissioned to show the horrific consequences of motor vehicle accidents were having the perverse effect, particularly in young men, of making them seem glamorous and heroic. What such advertisements lacked, the Brechtian would say, is precisely this dimension of the estrangement effect, which produces thought rather than pathos or worse yet more mental numbness.

19 Jameson offers his own account of these processes in *PCL*, 350.

20 In this context, Jameson's attraction to Brecht stands revealed in the

peculiar angle of his own approach to Lenin – he reads Lenin as a theorist
of the counter-revolution, that is, of the constant threat of the backward
slide towards the 'dirty pleasures' of capitalism socialism had constantly to
confront. I am referring here to an unpublished paper Jameson gave at a
2002 conference on Lenin in Essen, Germany, convened by Slavoj Žižek.

21 It should be added, of course, that Barthes did not become pro-Right for
being anti-Left, rather he moved in the direction of the neither/nor of the
apolitical.

22 Jameson adopts this slogan in his book on utopia (*AF*, xvi).

23 As Jameson suggests elsewhere (*PU*, 27), Hegel is effectively a codeword for
Stalin for the French Left of the 1960s and 1970s.

24 R. Barthes, *The Pleasure of the Text* (trans. R. Miller; NY: Hill and Wang,
1975) p. 17.

Chapter 3

The Political Unconscious

> Interpretation is not an isolated act, but takes place within a Homeric battlefield, on which a host of interpretive options are either openly or implicitly in conflict.
>
> Fredric Jameson, *The Political Unconscious*

The Political Unconscious is the first plank in an as yet uncompleted, totalizing account of realism, modernism and postmodernism (only with respect to the last of these three periods have we perhaps been given a definitive statement, although even that is subject to revision as his new work on 'globalization' appears; his account of modernism is still very much a work in progress, while realism which seemed finished with this book has since been revived). Meanwhile, the concept of the 'political unconscious' and the complex, multilayered interpretive apparatus associated with it, which will be our primary focus in this chapter, should be regarded as the apotheosis and completion of the programme to develop a new form of dialectical criticism Jameson started to develop a decade earlier under the rubric of 'metacommentary'. It takes on board all the lessons learned over the years from numerous interlocutors (particularly Sartre, Adorno, Brecht and Barthes, as we saw in Chapter 2) and then raises it all to a higher power. But this is an apprehension of the book we must arrive at, rather than commence with, or else wipe from view its complex and highly polemical texture.

At the distance of a quarter of a century since its publication, it has however become difficult to see the extent to which *The Political Unconscious* is itself a 'Homeric battlefield' in which a host of literary theoretical options are 'either openly or implicitly in conflict'. Most of the battles it weighs into were won and lost years ago, leaving us to wonder – much as the astronauts do in *2001: A Space Odyssey* (Kubrick, 1969) when they discover the obelisk on the moon – what its polemical purpose was. To see this, and to understand the particular shape of the book we need to mentally reconstruct its context – first of all, it is Jameson's first major foray into the territory held and defended by English departments (it is easy to forget that Jameson's own 'disciplines' are French and comparative literature): the critique of Frye (as well as the extended readings of Gissing and Conrad) is an attack on the old guard of myth criticism; second of all, it is a reply to the forces of deconstruction rising up out of French departments and spilling into virtually all areas of the humanities, spreading its virulent strain of anti-historicism; thirdly, it is a settling of accounts with Althusser and Althusserianism, as much to clarify disagreements as to try to forge a *rapprochement* by highlighting the degree to which Althusser's apparatus can be accommodated by contemporary paradigms of literary criticism.

Fundamentally, though, *The Political Unconscious* is the elaboration of a method, but one whose lessons have only partially been absorbed and learned, even by its many adherents. Although it has become a standard component of literary theory's compendious 'toolbox', it knows a life and fate largely independent of its creator. Jameson's slogan, 'Always historicize!', with which *The Political Unconscious* famously opens, means something rather more than simply reading texts in their historical context, yet this is very often how it is understood. His purpose is not, for instance, either comparable or compatible with the New Historicist project initiated by Stephen Greenblatt and Walter Benn Michaels, among others, even though at first glance there might appear to be some obvious affinities.[1] The difference, and it is a large one, is that their relative conceptions of history are utterly at odds. New Historicism is committed to a subject-centred view of history. It is concerned with the intriguing texture of specific lives. It exhumes the objects and documents, public records and private memoirs, of a distant past to fashion a montage (Jameson's word) of details creating the illusion of interiority, very much in the manner of cinema, thereby giving us a vivid sense of what it must have felt like to be that person. But it is an hallucination. By assembling the everyday items some historical figure or other, Shakespeare or Marlowe say, must have been surrounded by, must have routinely used or thought about, the historian's 'eye' begins to seem as though it is mimicking the subject's 'I' and the illusion is formed. We feel as though we are seeing 'their' world in the same way 'they' did and as a consequence 'they' always seem more modern than we expected 'them' to be.

Jameson, in contrast, is committed to an object-centred view of history in which private lives are lived in confrontation with the deeper drama of what Marxism terms the mode of production, which refers to the manner and means of generating and distributing wealth on a social scale. He rejects those histories which continue to believe (as New Historicism plainly does) that social and cultural change can be grasped phenomenologically, from the perspective of a single individual, and argues in favour of a philosophy of history which can come to grips with what he calls the 'scandal' of social and cultural change, which always comes from the outside and in a form that is beyond sense (*PU*, 26). The only philosophy of history capable of satisfying that demand, Jameson argues, is Marxism.

> To imagine that, sheltered from the omnipresence of history and the implacable influence of the social, there already exists a realm of freedom – whether it be that of the microscopic experience of words in a text or the ecstasies and intensities of the various private religions – is only to strengthen the grip of Necessity over all such blind zones in which the individual seeks refuge, in pursuit of a purely individual, a merely psychological, project of salvation. The only effective liberation from such constraint begins with the recognition that there is nothing that is not social and historical – indeed, that everything is 'in the last analysis' political. (*PU*, 20)

'Only Marxism', he writes, 'can give us an adequate account of the essential *mystery* of the cultural past, which, like Tiresias drinking the blood, is momentarily returned to life and warmth and allowed once more to speak, and to deliver its long forgotten message in surroundings utterly alien to it' (*PU*, 19).[2] Only Marxism situates the individual life 'within the unity of a single great collective story', namely the 'collective struggle to wrest a realm of Freedom from a realm of Necessity' (*PU*, 19). The principal polemical purpose of the work, then, is to 'argue the priority of a Marxian interpretive framework', but not as one might expect by arguing against other interpretative frameworks in a combative spirit and knocking them out of contention (which is not to say, however, that he does not do precisely that, namely argue against other interpretative frameworks, only that this is not his principal aim, nor indeed his principal strategy). His strategy is rather bolder, and indeed rather more combative, than that. Jameson proposes to subsume all the other interpretative frameworks by subsuming them under one single, 'untranscendable horizon', that of Marxism itself (*PU*, 10, 47). His point, as *Marxism and Form* instructed us a decade earlier, is that 'Marxism is not just one more theory of history, but on the contrary the "end" or abolition of theories of history as such' (*MF*, 321). Jameson's rationale, which stems at least as much from his commitment to Marxism *tout court* as his guerrilla-like sense of which battles are worth fighting and which are not, is that taken on their own terms, the more prominent interpretative frameworks of the latter half of the twentieth century (structuralism, post-structuralism, deconstruction, but also New Historicism, postmodernism and so on) are basically unassailable. So strong is the local validity of the diverse set of theoretical discourses operating under the mantle of 'theory', Marxism cannot be defended 'as a mere substitute', as a better choice in this or that instance. The 'authority of such methods springs from their faithful consonance with this or that local law of a fragmented life' (the condition that – as we saw in Chapter 2 – Jameson elsewhere terms 'nominalism'), which is to say their local authority springs from the fact that they actively repudiate the possibility of a greater, more encompassing viewpoint (*PU*, 10).

The Political Unconscious can in this sense be read as a defence of abstraction, which is something it has in common with all of Jameson's books before and since. This is the one battle fought out in the pages of *The Political Unconscious* that continues to be relevant to its contemporary readership because ours still seems to be an age 'when people no longer understand what dialectical thinking is or why the dialectic came into being in the first place, when they have abandoned the dialectic for less rewarding Nietzschean positions' (*IFJ*, 93). I would want to add, though, that to the extent that the present admiration for Deleuze's work is responsible for this shift, it stems from a misreading of Deleuze – after all, he famously said the only problem posed by abstraction is the problem of not being abstract enough. But the greater responsibility for this shift probably lies with Lyotard, whose emblematic slogan 'incredulity towards metanarratives' is precisely directed against Marxism.[3] His strategy in *The Postmodern Condition* is to undermine Marxism by opposing the very possibility of any theory (not just Marxism) attaining a position of universality, thus shattering ahead of time any ambition Marxism might have of proposing 'a single great collective story'.[4] The crisis Lyotard diagnoses (the loss of the ideologically cohesive – but pernicious – power of metanarratives) can be resolved, Jameson suggests, by positing 'not the disappearance of the great master narratives, but their passage underground as it were, their continuing but now *unconscious* effectivity as a way of "thinking about" and acting in our current situation' (*F2*, xii). This is why Jameson argues for the *priority* of the Marxist position – what he means to say is that such disenchanted positions as Lyotard's take their place as so many 'provinces' on a 'plane of immanence' always already staked out by Marxism. On this view,

Marxism is not a rival of structuralism, post-structuralism, deconstruction and so forth because it is not a contemporary; it is, rather, their condition of possibility, regardless of their affiliation or not with Marx. Thus, while we may sympathize with Cornel West when he says that Jameson should have said post-structuralism's and deconstruction's critiques of history are wrong rather than misplaced, it should be clear who the better strategist is.[5]

History

'The type of interpretation' Jameson proposes under the rubric of 'political unconscious' may be grasped, he suggests, as 'the rewriting of the literary text in such a way that the latter may itself be seen as the rewriting or restructuration of a prior historical or ideological *subtext*, it being always understood that that "subtext" is not immediately present as such' but must itself be '(re)constructed after the fact' (*PU*, 81). Interpretation is, in this sense, an essentially allegorical act with history standing in the place of the master text. This is meant quite literally – allegory is the model of reading/rewriting texts underpinning the entirety of the project going by the name of 'political unconscious'. Allegory is a pivotal concept for Jameson, he relies on it a great deal, but his use of it is idiosyncratic, idiosyncratic enough to trouble even Derrida.[6] What Jameson has in mind, then, when he says 'allegory' is not at all the traditional conception of it as a type of text for which a well-formed key, traditionally the Bible, exists that can unlock a fixed set of hidden meanings from an apparently fluid set of surface appearances. In the hands of the knowing, texts like *The Chronicles of Narnia* immediately yield a clear-cut set of Christian messages, even though to the unknowing it may appear to be just another pagan tale of witches and elves. This is because the story contains a number of relatively standardized themes, such as self-sacrifice and holy resurrection, which owe their origins to the Bible. Therefore, providing one is familiar with them, they can be seen as creative transfigurations of Bible stories. But, and this is the crucial point, to rewrite *Narnia* in such a way as to foreground its master text, namely the Bible, requires that one know the Bible to begin with. If one is ignorant of such matters, a study of the Bible will soon remedy things – in effect, the knowledge needed to decode the allegorical text of this type is always to hand. If, as Jameson does, one substitutes history for the Bible and conceives that as the master text, then obviously enough the allegorical process of reading/rewriting becomes a quite different and altogether uncertain prospect.[7] The effect of this manoeuvre is to transform the master text from a solution back into a problematic.

History is another one of those codewords, like allegory, that Jameson relies on throughout his work, attributing to it his own specific set of valences. History is the ultimate master code, for Jameson, the one code that decodes all codes – it is in this sense what philosophers call a 'ground', a facility which thought, and indeed textuality, rely on without directly expressing it (i.e., our grounds for believing in God, say, are not of the same order as our actual belief in God, which is why it is possible – some would even say it is necessary – to believe in God despite having no grounds to do so). But history is obviously not just a hermeneutic key of keys, it is 'what really happens', the record of events great and small, and in this sense it is what philosophers call a 'cause', albeit an 'absent cause' inasmuch as it is only ever felt through its effects (*PU*, 35). History in this latter sense, which is the predominant sense in which Jameson uses it, is a codeword for necessity, for that which 'must be'. We must eat, we must have shelter, we must have clean water, we must make ourselves safe from predators, and so on, and all these musts have to be wrought from a nature indifferent to our existence, a pitiless nature that will inflict hot and cold weather upon us, feast or famine, flood or fire, regardless of how well we are prepared to cope with it, regardless indeed of whether it will cause us to live or die.[8] It is the inexorability of history (understood as this endless confrontation with an implacable nature), which grounds our thought, giving it the richness and reality of life itself. Jameson maintains that only Marxism is capable of thinking history in this way, as a vital force whose powers can still be felt even when it passes into textual form.

> History is what hurts, it is what refuses desire and sets inexorable limits to individual as well as collective praxis, which its 'ruses' turn into grisly and ironic reversals of their overt intention. But this history can be apprehended only through its effects, and never directly as some reified force. This is indeed the ultimate sense in which History as ground and untranscendable horizon needs no particular justification: we may be sure that its alienating necessities will not forget us, however much we might prefer to ignore them. (*PU*, 102)

For Jameson (contra Derrida) history *is* outside the text, and indeed the outside of text, yet (in partial agreement with Derrida) only accessible to us in textual form and therefore very much inside the text too. This is the essential paradox the concept of the political unconscious must resolve.

Jameson resolves this paradox of a history that is simultaneously ground and cause in two ways: first, he argues that all texts embody history in their form; second, he argues that texts are in themselves historical events, albeit events that take place on a symbolic or unconscious plane. The first argument was set in place ten years earlier in the program essay on method called 'Metacommentary' (as we saw in Chapter 1). It is developed further here along the lines that all texts draw history inwards as their necessary subtext. The second argument was given preliminary figuration in *Marxism and Form*, but receives its fullest treatment with this work (*MF*, 383). Another illuminating foretaste of it was given in the 1979 essay, 'Reification and Utopia in Mass Culture' first published in the inaugural issue of *Social Text*, a journal Jameson co-founded, and later reprinted in *Signatures of the Visible*.[9] The model for this move is adapted from Claude Lévi-Strauss's structural analysis of Caduveo facial decoration, and augmented by Norman Holland's suggestive reworking of Freud's concept of censorship.

The crucial proposition that catches Jameson's eye is found in the following quotation he cites from Lévi-Strauss's great autobiographical work, *Tristes Tropiques*: the graphic art of the Caduveo women is to be interpreted, Lévi-Strauss believes, as 'the fantasy production of a society seeking passionately to give symbolic expression to the institutions it might have had in reality, had not interest and superstition stood in the way' (*PU*, 79). Unable, or perhaps unwilling, to change its social institutions, some of which it experiences as unbearable, the Caduveo fabricate symbolic solutions to the real contradictions of existence through their body art. Haunted by what Lévi-Strauss himself refers to as a 'golden age', but which we may re-write in more Jamesonian terms as simply 'utopia', the Caduveo project and valorize this 'other' place via their ornamentation and art.[10] Jameson's hypothesis is that contemporary western society is in essence the same inasmuch as it too is haunted by a utopia it can neither access nor dismiss. 'We may suggest', Jameson muses, 'that from this perspective, ideology is not something which informs or invests symbolic production; rather the aesthetic act is itself ideological, and the production of aesthetic or narrative form is to be seen as an ideological act in its own right, with the function of inventing imaginary or formal "solutions" to unresolvable social contradictions' (*PU*, 79).

The place where this process of working out symbolic solutions to real problems is most visible in contemporary aesthetic production is political allegory, the operation of which Jameson is able to discover in the most surprising of places (*PU*, 80). In the 1979 essay mentioned above, 'Reification and Utopia in Mass Culture', Jameson provides a memorable demonstration of how this particular proposition might play itself out as a means of analysing contemporary cultural production. He takes as his example the then quite recent blockbuster *Jaws* (Spielberg, 1975), based on the best-selling thriller of the same name by Peter Benchley which tells the story of a summer season gone awry in a small town on the ironically named fictional island of Amity. An early example of what film historians would come to call the 'New Hollywood', a sweeping rubric that includes the work of Francis Ford Coppola, Steven Spielberg, George Lucas, William Friedkin and Brian De Palma, among others, *Jaws* has received a lot of critical attention for being at once an excitingly well made film, that is, a film with real directorial flair, and a huge mass market success.[11] Academically, though, the key concern has always been what does the shark at the centre of the story actually stand for? Speculation on this issue has ranged, as Jameson records, from predictable psychoanalytic attempts to decode it as representing the phallus, to more historically conscious and politically charged readings of it as an allegory of US imperialism. It was even rumoured that Fidel Castro interpreted Amity as standing for Cuba and the shark US imperialism (*SV*, 232 n. 12). None of these readings 'can be said to be wrong or aberrant', Jameson admits, 'but their very multiplicity suggests that the vocation of the symbol – the killer shark – lies less in any single message or meaning than its capacity to absorb and organise all of these quite distinct anxieties together' (*SV*, 26). By fixating on the problem of the meaning of the shark, by trying to decipher its symbolic import and assign it a definite figurative content, we miss its real vocation, which is to serve as a pretext for the working out of a quite complex set of social as well as class conflicts.[12]

The more interesting questions of a symbolic nature posed by the film have to do with what the key protagonists – the cop Brody (Roy Scheider), the scientist Hooper (Richard Dreyfus) and the shark-hunter Quint (Robert Shaw) – stand for. Jameson reads these figures as representations of both different social strata and different historical generations, with the result that the film is seen as a conflict between two Americas, with Brody and Hooper on the one hand representing the emergent 'post-modern' society (a combination of a militarized law enforcement and college-educated old money), and Quint on the other hand as the griz-zled representative of the now determinately outmoded America of the 'New Deal'.[13] Ultimately *Jaws* is read as:

> [The] allegory of an alliance between the forces of law-and-order
> and the new technocracy of multinational corporations: an alliance
> which must be cemented, not merely by the fantasised triumph over
> the ill-defined menace of the shark itself, but above all by the
> indispensable precondition of the effacement of that more trad-
> itional image of an older America which must be eliminated from
> historical consciousness and social memory before the new power
> system takes its place. (*SV*, 29)

One can readily detect here the background presence of Deleuze and
Guattari's famous slogan, 'don't ask what it means, ask how it works',
strategically cited and endorsed by Jameson in *The Political Unconscious*.
The interesting implication of this observation, which so far nobody has
commented on, is the question it raises about the degree to which
Deleuze and Guattari were influenced in their thinking by Lévi-Strauss's
formulation? Much more than they let on, one suspects, which would
tend to confirm Jameson's claim that their allegedly anti-interpretive
stance should simply be treated as a polemical announcement of a new
hermeneutic program (*PU*, 21–23). For Jameson, this new hermeneutic
program has as its vocation 'the unmasking of cultural artefacts as
socially symbolic acts' (*PU*, 20). This means revealing the degree to
which all texts are in fact political allegories, symbolically working
through and provisionally resolving a variety of social and cultural anxieties. What the example of *Jaws* shows, though, is that it doesn't matter
whether the text is actually or intentionally coded as an allegory, because
readers can always find a way of turning it into one – Jameson will go so
far as to say readers need to turn it into one in order to get interested in
it. All texts draw history inwards and offer it back to readers as a hermeneutic key, enabling them to find 'relevance' in even those texts which
like *Jaws* display no visible intent to be anything more than an absorbing
afternoon's entertainment.

Relevance, however, should not be confused with pluralism or its
cognate the 'open text' (see Jameson's critique of this notion in the
interview included in this volume). In contrast to someone like Catherine
Belsey, who argues that a Left politics is best served by a literary criticism
that underscores the plurality of readings any one text can be made to
yield, Jameson is arguing for a position that wants to uncover the singu-
larity of the situation in which the artist worked.[14] As we have seen in
relation to his discussion of *Jaws*, Jameson's argument is that ideology
masks its operation in the plurality of meanings it makes available, and
really comes into its own when it absorbs rather than emits meanings.

Therefore, if the critic's task is to unmask the diverse ways ideology conceals its own existence, as Belsey rightly says it is (following Althusser), then it is a peculiarly self-defeating ploy to devote one's critical energies to enhancing ideology's disguise by multiplying the interpretations of a text. The better strategy, which Jameson identifies as an allegorical mode of reading, is to try to trace the path of necessity and see why a text is written the way it is and what effects it obtains in consequence.

Allegory

There is perhaps no slipperier term than 'relevance' in the entire critical-theory arsenal. It is not one that Jameson himself favours, but I bring it in here as a way of introducing a second level of complexity to the foregoing discussion of Lévi-Strauss's idea that cultural texts can enact symbolic solutions to real social and cultural problems. For it is not enough to say that we can read all cultural texts as historical or political allegories, we also have to account for why we should *want to do so* in the first place. Part of the answer to this question has been given already. Unable or unwilling to change our situation, except at the most privative of levels, such as the condition of our body (but even there obvious constraints apply), 'relevant' cultural texts absorb our longing for difference, or what Jameson will later describe as 'the desire called utopia'. Thus, to solicit our interest, cultural texts must, albeit in some quite minimal way, hold out the promise of the real and indeed fully visceral pleasure of utopian transformation – this, for Jameson, as he explains in *Postmodernism, or, the Cultural Logic of Late Capitalism*, is the nature of the satisfaction to be obtained from apparently dystopian texts like *Mad Max* (Miller, 1979). The end of our world, however horrible it is to contemplate such an eventuality, nevertheless furnishes the occasion for the properly utopian imagining of its splendid reconstruction (*PCL*, 383–85). In the case of *Jaws* this utopian aspect reveals itself in its subtle, not to say flaccid, critique of existing society, which it portrays as empty headed and hedonistic on the one hand (the tourists, particularly the teenagers who do not heed the warnings to stay out of the water), and narrow minded and conservative on the other hand (the local townsfolk who are more concerned with profit margins than safety). Killing the shark is thus a pretext for a drama about the refashioning of social relations – teenagers have to learn to 'respect their elders' and the elders have to learn to put the lives of the teenagers ahead of business.[15] In their turn, these set-piece confrontations between the generations, as well as between the locals and the visitors, which always appear to impede the main action of the story but should in fact be seen *as the main story*, evoke more abstract concerns about personal freedom (the right to have the kind of fun we choose) and, just as importantly, security of livelihood (the threat of foreign competition on local jobs [i.e., the shark], the damaging effect of government regulation [i.e., the ban on swimming which threatens to ruin the tourist season]).

Jameson's thesis is that cultural texts provoke such anxieties as these in order to *manage* them. This, then, is the second level of complexity that Jameson adds to Lévi-Strauss's idea (borrowing from Norman Holland's *The Dynamics of Literary Response*). What the text must manage is precisely the dangerous and disruptive desire for change its utopian elements betoken. The text needs to do two contradictory kinds of work: it must solicit our interest by offering up the possibility of the quite real satisfaction of a genuinely changed society; it must then contain that desire by persuading it to be satisfied with the less than genuine symbolic change.

> For Holland, the psychic function of the work of art must be described in such a way that these two inconsistent and even incompatible features of aesthetic gratification – on the one hand, its wish-fulfilling function, but on the other the necessity that its symbolic structure protect the psyche against the frightening and potentially damaging eruption of powerful archaic desires and wish-material – be somehow harmonised and assigned their place as twin drives of a single structure. (*SV*, 25)

Uplifted as we may feel at the end *Jaws* when the shark is finally dead and the town seems ready to collectively heal itself, the sense of transformation we are responding to is illusory, even though our yearning for it is not. Not only is it simply a movie and not real life, the image of change it offers is false too – Amity is not changed, it is in a state of mourning following a very traumatic set of events. The story closes with a cessation of hostilities following the elimination of an external threat, but all it can muster in the way of real change is the pathos we feel when we recognize that if only we had acted differently, things might have turned out better than they did. Even after everything that has happened there, it is still a seaside resort town dependent on sun-seeking tourists; and it is still populated by the same narrow-minded townsfolk eager for the tourist dollar. The allegorical structure of *Jaws* both rouses and quenches the desire for change. As an interpretive model, then, what the political unconscious seeks to do is show the transformational labour performed by cultural texts as they simultaneously provoke and rework our cultural anxieties and fantasies (*SV*, 25). It does this by treating the text as a multilayered entity, with history serving as the ultimate horizon.

Jameson is by no means alone in adopting an allegorical model of reading/rewriting texts, although he is one of the very few to acknowledge it openly and not try to disguise it. In fact, one could say that virtually everything that goes by the name of literary theory in the latter half of the twentieth century is allegorical in structure (certainly this is the assumption underpinning Jameson's concept of the metacommentary [*IT2*, 149], which in this light can be seen as a comparative study of master texts). There is a subtle acknowledgement of the prevalence of allegorical structures in literary theory, albeit in the manner of a Freudian 'return of the repressed', in the habit of contemporary practitioners of it describing what they do when they read texts as 'exegesis', a word which traditionally refers to comparative analysis of the Bible, usually with an eye toward determining which is the most 'reliable' version, given the vagaries of its many translations. This choice of word and the allusion to biblical studies it implies offers its own lesson if we focus on the fact that 'exegesis' would not be needed if the Bible existed in a completely stable form. Patently, it does not. As a text that was written by many different authors, over hundreds of years, and in three different languages, it is very far from having a stable form, and that is even before we take into account the instability of the long and, not always happy, process of translation it has been subjected to, which has seen it pass from ancient languages to classical languages to vernacular languages.

Setting aside doctrinal issues and concentrating only on the textual issues, what is instructive for our purposes here is the fact that the Bible as master text is not pre-existing, it too has been constructed, and just as importantly knows its own master text, its own projected ideal which scholars use as a yardstick to measure the degree of fidelity one version of the Bible exhibits compared with another. The 'real' of the Bible, then, the one 'true' version we can rely upon to settle all disputes is in fact as much of a construction as any one of the hundreds of actually existing versions of the Bible, which by contrast are in some small way or other compromised, or imperfect against this projected ideal. It is a construction enacted and promoted by the actually existing Bibles, which always present themselves as striving towards this ideal.

History can be pressed into service in the same way – its stories, which will always seem to belong to the past, may just as well be contemporary creations produced according to the demands of the present. More importantly, the uncertainty we have with respect to our history is no impediment to it functioning as a master text, as some ultimate interpretive horizon, because master texts are always already constructions – they can function *as* absolutes without necessarily having to *be* absolutes. If we follow the logic of this thread of an idea, that contemporary texts produce history according to their own needs, we come to what is undoubtedly Jameson's boldest idea: the text is an historical act in its own right. 'The literary or aesthetic act', he writes, 'always entertains some active relationship with the Real; yet in order to do so, it cannot simply allow "reality" to persevere inertly in its own being, outside the text and at distance. It must rather draw the Real into its own texture, and the ultimate paradoxes and false problems of linguistics, and most notably semantics, are to be traced back to this process, whereby language manages to carry the Real within itself as its own intrinsic or immanent subtext' (*PU*, 81). Texts never simply represent history, they intervene in history. They can do this because history itself is not a fixed and changeless entity, but a dynamic and rhizomatic process (to use Deleuze and Guattari's vivid concept) connecting the myriad present to the myriad past.

The operative word here is 'connect'. History joins the dots, it makes visible to us the abstract and intangible forces shaping daily life whose effects we feel even when we cannot see them. Think of the way the multifarious little acts of the bureaucratic institutions of law and justice, but also health and education, penetrate our social being. Mostly they come to us in the form of 'messages' whose origin and purpose we can never quite fathom – who, exactly, is it who worries that I drive too fast, drink too much, eat the wrong foods and do not get enough exercise? (*PU*, 81–82).[16] If the Health Department wants me to be 'healthy' (a state of my being it defines for me) it is not because it 'cares' for me, it is because my lack of health is costly – a drain on resources here, a loss of productivity there. This, as Foucault's great histories of the clinic and the prison have shown, is what history unearths, namely the connections between 'me' and the social machine 'I' am enmeshed in.

In changing how we see the past, by making the past alive to us in some fresh and problematic way, texts change how we situate ourselves in the present, they unsettle us. All texts have this potential to discomfit, even those we like to deride as 'schlock', such as airport thrillers and under-the-counter pulps, because they all must somehow and in their own way produce the 'Real'. Yet inasmuch as they achieve this, they also tend to erase that pre-existing real from our consciousness because to be reminded of it too often or too forcefully is to shatter the illusion of the real it projects. A text cannot feel real to us if it constantly reminds us of its unreality, therefore texts do not so much rely on history as rival it.

> The whole paradox of what we have here called the subtext may be summed up in this, that the literary work or cultural object, as though for the first time, brings into being that very situation to which it is also, at one and the same time, a reaction. It articulates its own situation and textualizes it, thereby encouraging and perpetu- ating the illusion that the situation itself did not exist before it, that there is nothing but a text, that there never was any extra- or con- textual reality before the text itself generated it in the form of a mirage. (*PU*, 81–82)

Thus we may say texts not only have a history, they make history too. It is this duality that Jameson wants to articulate.

Interpretation

The basic idea of the political unconscious is that if interpretation in terms of 'allegorical master narratives remains a constant temptation, this is because such master narratives have inscribed themselves in the text as well as in our thinking about them; such allegorical narrative signifieds are a persistent dimension of literary and cultural texts pre- cisely because they reflect a fundamental dimension of our collective thinking and our collective fantasies about history and reality' (*PU*, 34). As was said at the outset, the 'political unconscious' is a complex, multi- layered interpretive apparatus – it can now be seen to rest on the follow- ing four propositions: all cultural texts are political allegories; allegory is a cultural means of symbolically working through real social and cul- tural anxieties; only those texts which touch a nerve of genuine social and cultural concern will be interesting to us; and history is the ambiva- lent master code that enables us to decode the psychically and politically significant elements of a text. To enable us to see how a text is able to do all these things at once, in spite of the sometimes contradictory nature of the respective operations, Jameson proposes a three-tiered model of reading that conceives the reading process as a dynamic sequence of interpretations and re-interpretations (we might also say, constructions and re-constructions), which successively broaden the horizon of the textual engagement and transform the textual object itself such that in the end one has gone from dealing with a single work to dealing with the mode of production in its entirety. In the process the solid form of the text dissolves and appears in its true form as a highly compromised, but nonetheless creatively achieved, tissue of gestures and effects. The three tiers or horizons of interpretation and re-interpretation are:

1. Textual
2. Social
3. Mode of production

Each of these horizons has its own object of analysis: the first deals the with text as a 'symbolic act'; the second with something Jameson calls the 'ideologeme', which he defines as 'the smallest intelligible unit of the essentially antagonistic collective discourses of the social classes'; and the third has to do with the 'ideology of form' (*PU*, 76). The first horizon is the one we have largely been concerned with up until now. In spite of ourselves we cannot help but start with the single text, it being as much as we can read at any one time, unless of course we have that useful facility of being able to watch fifty or so televisions at once that David Bowie has in *The Man Who Fell to Earth* (Roeg, 1976). But we have to tutor ourselves to see beyond the illusion of self-sufficiency most texts promote and recognize their intrinsic structural dependency on the wider net of discourse. A single text is by itself semantically poor and read in isolation virtually meaningless.

History, Jameson argues, provides texts with the semantic enrichment needed to make them significant at the most elementary level. The three horizons he proposes are, in this precise sense, indices of an increase in the level of semantic enrichment achieved by folding more history into the mix, or, in other words, massively expanding the range and density of connections that can be made between a single text and the dis-cursive universe of which it is only ever but one 'utterance' among many. The object of analysis of this first horizon, the 'symbolic act', must be seen, Jameson stresses, as an estrangement of the standard item of interest of most models of textual analysis, namely 'the text', because in contrast to that relatively static and basically inert entity, it is a socially dynamic and indeed socially pragmatic event. Caduveo face painting is Jameson's basic model of what he means by 'symbolic act' and as we have seen this gives rise to a set of images that cannot simply be 'read'. Their meaning derives from the way they provide a figuration of actual social and cultural anxieties, which are largely to do with the iniquities of entrenched social hierarchies, and in giving expression to them seem to resolve or at least contain them. Our first apprehension of the text so conceived is as a symbolic solution to a real social and cultural problem whose dimensions and conditions we do not yet know. Deconcealing this problem is, we can now say, the practical meaning of the otherwise empty injunction to read texts in their historical context, mouthed by the party faithful of almost every faction of 'theory' in operation today.

What is empty about the enjoinment to read a text in its historical context is, I hasten to add, the sheer vacancy of the underlying concept of 'historical context', which for the most part means little more than knowing what life was like 'back then' and using that to manufacture what Greenblatt calls 'just-so' explanations, typically the pairing of real life events with details in the text – a mother's red dress becoming a son's taste for colour.[17] But history so conceived is merely so much data and cannot enable us to perceive the text in its true light as a 'symbolic act'. What is needed, rather, is some better sense of the problems and contradictions underpinning daily life, the problems and contradictions that arise from the socially elaborated differences between use value and exchange value, the alienating effect of the commodification of labour, the discrepant distribution of wealth under a market system, and so forth. Such 'problems' are not always visible to the naked eye, indeed such 'problems' can sometimes appear as their exact opposite.

Think of the perverse way in which 'flexible' jobs were first created to meet the needs of a particular section of the workforce, primarily women with children who have to work within the constraints of the limited availability of childcare and the inflexibility of the school schedule, but has since become a reflexive solution for employers wanting to drive down their labour costs. Flexibility was granted, but at the awful cost of it becoming the norm rather than an exception. What looked like a victory for labour soon revealed itself as a defeat. Marxism's word for situations like this, in which a defeat appears as a victory, is 'false consciousness'. Over the years this concept has come under attack, particularly from Anglo-American cultural studies, which objects to what it perceives to be its dumbing down of subjects, so its continued usefulness needs to be defended. Some of the leading lights of the field have responded to the concept of 'false consciousness' as though it were a culture-wide accusation of stupidity, rather than a diagnosis of a state of incomplete understanding of history's true circumstances – the well-meaning labour activists who fought for 'flexible' working conditions could not have known how their victory would be used against them, thus there is no injustice or denigration in saying what they thought they knew was false. If there is a painful lesson to be learned from this particular case history it is doubtless that the destruction of 'real jobs' and their subsequent conversion into what Naomi Klein has aptly called McJobs through the process now known barbarously enough as 'flexibilization' occurred because labour as a whole did not unite against it.[18]

Cultural studies rejects 'false consciousness' on the grounds that today's consumers are savvy enough to know when they are being manipulated by advertising – if this is true, and we have every reason to think it is, then 'false consciousness' is indeed the wrong word. The better concept would be 'cynicism'. But knowing that an advertisement is a con is not the same thing as 'knowing' that the system as a whole is a con – one can live with the knowledge of the former, but knowledge of the latter is rather more distressing because it means having to come to terms with the fact that even the 'good things' are a rebuke. In liking my job, for instance, I have to swallow the fact that the state paying my salary is the very same state that colluded with George W. Bush to manufacture a case for war against Iraq and subsequently prosecute that war. It is also the same state that provides my children's education. Given that it is one and the same entity, I cannot endorse the latter (the good state that sponsors education) and indict the former (the bad state that sponsors war) without contradiction. Neither can I console myself with the disingenuous compromise that the state is basically good, but has a few bad parts to it, without dishonesty because I know this not to be true. I must also avoid the 'sad passion' (to use Spinoza's concept) of paranoia, namely the opposite idea to the previous one, that in effect the state is basically bad, but has a few good points, because this is disabling. It makes cynicism appear justified. Short of a revolution, what can one do but take a fatalistic view of things?

> The dilemma is intensified when we deny ourselves, as we just have, the solution of a coexistence of different functions, as when, for instance, it is suggested that the greatness of a given writer may be separated from his deplorable opinions, and is achieved in spite of them or even against them. Such a separation is possible only for a world-view – liberalism – in which the political and the ideological are mere secondary or 'public' adjuncts to the content of a real 'private' life, which is alone authentic and genuine. (*PU*, 289)

The whole of what we call ideology is geared toward containing inhospitable knowledge of the former type and promoting illusions of the latter variety. In short, Marxist history is not the accumulation of data; it is the production of knowledge as the overcoming of the twin 'evils' of false consciousness and cynicism.

What we refer to as historical context is misconceived if it is not seen in these terms as an incoherent set of implacable problems confronting every artist, challenging them to find some way of not only representing the problems but resolving them too, at least in a symbolic sense. This viewpoint must, in its turn, change how we conceive the text.

> When properly used, the concept of the 'text' does not, as in garden-variety semiotic practice today, 'reduce' these realities to small and manageable written documents of one kind or another, but rather liberates us from the empirical object – whether institution, event, or individual work – by displacing our attention to its *constitution* as an object and its *relationship* to the other objects thus constituted. (*PU*, 297)

The text bears the trace of these realities and it is our job as critics to examine texts for all such signs of history's hidden hand. Perhaps the most basic lesson here is that the text is not the singular output of some isolated genius working in ignorance of society. But we should be wary of compounding the error by turning it around and saying the work of art reflects society. As Jameson reminds us, the work of art 'certainly reflects something, but what it reflects is not so much the class in itself as some autonomous cultural configuration, as rather the situation of that class, or, in short, class conflict' (*MF*, 382). We should be just as sceptical then of those critical or textual practices which – overtly or covertly – perpetuate the myth of the stand-alone text as those which want to see the text as holding up a mirror to society (as Lacan demonstrated, mirrors promote their own kind of 'false consciousness', specifically 'misrecognition'). The text is always and irreducibly what Deleuze and Guattari call a 'collective enunciation', which is to say a statement that can only be understood in social terms. This brings us to the second horizon, which Jameson defines as the social horizon, the horizon of class consciousness and the ideologeme. 'On this rewriting, the individual utterance or text is grasped as a symbolic move in an essentially polemic and strategic ideological confrontation between the classes, and to describe it in these terms (or to reveal it in this form) demands a whole set of different instruments' (*PU*, 85). If the text was first conceived as a symbolic solution to the structural problems of history, it must now be reconceived in dialogue with another class fraction (it being understood that class is inherently a relational concept) whose voice we have – perhaps – since forgotten. But to do this in a satisfactory manner we need some new way of articulating class discourse: it is to this end that Jameson invents the notion of the ideologeme.

> The ideologeme is an amphibious formation, whose essential structural characteristic may be described as its possibility to manifest itself as a pseudoidea – a conceptual or belief system, an abstract value, an opinion or prejudice – or as a protonarrative, a kind of ultimate class fantasy about the 'collective characters' which are the classes in opposition. (*PU*, 87)

'This duality', Jameson continues, means that 'it must be susceptible to both a conceptual description and a narrative manifestation all at once' (*PU*, 87). Jameson's prime exhibit in this regard is the nineteenth-century notion of *ressentiment*, 'of which Nietzsche was the primary theorist, if not, indeed, the metaphysician' (*PU*, 201). Nietzsche's position, as Jameson sees it, is that 'ethics in general and the Judeo-Christian tradition in particular [is] a revenge of the slaves upon the masters and an ideological ruse whereby the former infect the latter with a slave mentality – the ethos of charity – in order to rob them of their natural vitality and aggressive, properly aristocratic values' (*PU*, 201). *Ressentiment* is the standard nineteenth-century explanation for lower-class disenchantment with the state of things. It finds new life today in such slogans of the Right as 'self reliance' which hold that the poor are only poor because they do not have the character to change their situation. The same line of thinking is to be found in the nonsense idea that welfare is bad for poor people because it undermines their passion and drive to find work and lift themselves out of the 'poverty cycle' (a Left liberal term that in its own way is equally heartless since it contents itself with the idea that poverty is inexorable). These slogans show quite clearly that, as Jameson argues, the profoundest instances of *ressentiment* are always to be found on the side of the diagnostician rather than the sufferers. It is not the ones who are said to be afflicted by *ressentiment* that actually have it; it is rather the ones doing the finger-pointing who are the most blighted. But, and this is Jameson's real point, the diagnosis of *ressentiment* is simply a precondition for the negation of politics by recasting it in terms of ethics. By rewriting poverty as a character flaw and debating welfare in terms of whether it is good or bad for the character of the poor, the reality that poverty is a structural condition and effect of capitalism is blotted from view. *Ideologiekritik* today means unmasking ideologemes like this.

The third horizon places the social formation of the previous horizon within a species level frame, encompassing human history as a whole. It concerns, then, not a single mode of production, but all modes of production, or more precisely the comparative friction between modes of production. 'We will therefore suggest that this new and ultimate object may be designated, drawing on recent historical experience, as *cultural revolution*, that moment in which the coexistence of various modes of production become visibly antagonistic, their contradictions moving to the very centre of political, social, and historical life' (*PU*, 95; *MF*, 91). The 'incomplete Chinese experiment' (as Jameson calls it) is but one example of a general condition whose other exemplars might include such long durée events as the western Enlightenment, which as is well known enacted a powerful transformation of European habits of mind and culture. Secularization is perhaps the strongest form of cultural revolution so far known to history. But, Jameson cautions, this view of things is distorting inasmuch as it makes it appear that cultural revolutions only occur in those rare transitional moments in history during which one cultural dominant supersedes another. The reality is that such moments are 'but the passage to the surface of a permanent process in human societies, of a permanent struggle between the various coexisting modes of production' (*PU*, 97).

The critic's task is to rewrite the text in such a way that this uninterrupted cultural revolution 'can be apprehended and read as the deeper and more permanent constitutive structure in which the empirical textual objects know intelligibility' (*PU*, 97). This task is realized most fully in the elaboration of what Jameson elsewhere calls 'periodising hypotheses' (postmodernism being Jameson's own quite famous example), which in their strongest form have the effect of producing new abstractions with which to 'think' an age. But this is only one half of the process. We still need to specify an object able to vehiculate such a hypothesis. The object of this third and indeed ultimate horizon is '*the ideology of form*, that is, the determinate contradiction of the specific messages emitted by the varied sign systems which coexist in a given artistic process as well as in its general social formation' (*PU*, 98). The critic's royal road to explicating 'the ideology of form' is genre – the implication not to be missed here, as Žižek likes to say, is that genre is transformed into an index of period.

> Thus, the deviation of the individual text from some deeper narrative structure directs our attention to those determinate changes in the historical situation which block a full manifestation or

replication of the structure on the discursive level. On the other hand, the failure of a particular generic structure, such as epic, to reproduce itself not only encourages a search for those substitute textual formations that appear in its wake, but more particularly alerts us to the historical ground, now no longer existent, in which the original structure was meaningful. (*PU*, 146)

This, at any rate, is how we must now think of genre. Jameson's reconceptualization of genre which follows from this proposition is undoubtedly one of the major reasons why *The Political Unconscious* became the landmark text it did. Genres live and die according to how well they stage and symbolically resolve the social and cultural anxieties of their time. This claim can also be read in the other direction as a theory of change, about which Jameson himself offers the following edict: 'no genuinely or radically different culture can emerge without a radical modification of the social system from which culture itself springs' (*SV*, 161). His theorization of postmodernism will follow exactly this path: it is the transformations in late capitalism itself that have given rise to a new cultural logic, which he proposes to call postmodernism. Thus, 'even if all the constitutive features of postmodernism were identical with and coterminous to those of an older modernism . . . the two phenomena would still remain utterly distinct in their meaning and social function, owing to the very different positioning of postmodernism in the economic system of late capital and, beyond that, to the transformation of the very sphere of culture in contemporary society' (*PCL*, 5).

The linking of genre and cultural revolution serves to remind us that genre is not necessarily benign or innocent. The essential task of all cultural revolutions is the reprogramming of entrenched cultural attitudes, particularly the perhaps-centuries-old habits of subalternity all cultures accrue like effluvium from the great wash of history, along with what is sometimes referred to as 'the willingness to submit', a psychologism supposed to explain why we put up with intolerable political regimes for as long as we do.[19] Such reprogramming is not without its ambivalences. Nazism was without question one of the most successful cultural revolutions of all time, it resulted in the most severe and indeed frightening changes in cultural attitudes witnessed in recent history.

These transformations were inherently paradoxical: subservience to the general order of the regime was won by promoting disorder at every other level – you can do what you want, you can rape, kill and maim the enemy in whatever obscene fashion you like, just so long as you give your allegiance to the regime, was Nazism's basic message. It conveyed this message via one of the most potent ideologemes invented, the concept of 'right' – it said: you, as German citizen, have a right to global sovereignty, but that right, which until now has been denied you by a global conspiracy of Jews, has to be protected by force and this is what Nazism pledges to you it will do, even if we have to kill everyone to do it. Here the pseudoidea of a right to global sovereignty (manufactured from myths of racial superiority) and the protonarrative of a global conspiracy denying that right (a confection of old hatreds and a need to blame someone for impoverished economic conditions) combined powerfully to produce one of the most stirring calls to action in recorded history. Not surprisingly, the regime's favoured genre was tragedy. From the beginning, 'the Nazis announced to Germany what they were bringing: at once wedding bells and death, including their own death, and the death of the Germans. They thought they would perish but that their undertaking would be resumed, all across Europe, all over the world, throughout the solar system. And the people cheered, not because they did not understand, but because they wanted that death through the death of others.'[20]

Genre is a social contract between a writer and an intended public, specifying the proper use of a text. In its strong form, as in the work of Northrop Frye, genre bears witness to the great sacralizing archetypes of diurnal existence, the tropes and symbols of nature that rhizomatically connect up 'to unify and integrate our literary experience'.[21] Genre in this sense is literature's means of communicating with itself and our means of communicating back, but this notion depends on the continued existence of a close-bound community of readers and writers of the type that used to be known as 'schools' (in English literature, no doubt the Bloomsbury group is the best known). 'The greatness of Frye', Jameson asserts, 'lies in his willingness to raise the issue of community and to draw basic, essentially social, interpretive consequences from the nature of religion as collective representation' (*PU*, 69). But in a market system such as ours in which the intended public is increasingly fragmented and dispersed such essentially legislative aspirations are growing harder and harder to contemplate, let alone enforce.

Commodification turns genre into a brand-name (in the final form of this process the brand-name supplants the genre itself, as Mills and Boon has done in the case of romance) and the social contract into a product guarantee. Under such conditions it is the reader who dictates terms to the writer, leaving genre to live out a half-life (as Jameson puts it) as a drug-store and airport-lounge product line. It would thus seem

necessary, Jameson concludes, that we 'invent a new, historically reflexive, way of using categories, such as those of genre, which are so clearly
implicated in the literary history and the formal production they were
traditionally supposed to classify and neutrally to describe' (*PU*, 107).
This reinvention should be enacted along what might be described as a
faultline in contemporary approaches to genre, which exhibits two main
tendencies, designated by Jameson as semantic and syntactic, that are
only apparently in opposition. Frye's work, which conceives genre as a
mode, a kind of ideal entity differently embodied in a host of texts,
offers the most developed form of the first variety, Jameson suggests,
while Russian Formalism, particularly the work of folktale morphologist
Vladimir Propp, who conceives genre as a fixed form, is the most
developed form of the second variety. This distinction reprises the
Deleuzian antagonism between a model of interpretation that asks what
a text means and an anti-interpretive model that asks how a text works
(*PU*, 69).

What Jameson proposes in effect is to historicize the mental category
of genre and he does this by reading back into Frye and Propp that
which they purposely exclude. This is achieved by problematizing, in the
historical sense of the word we have examined above, the category's
constitutive presuppositions. In the case of Frye this means problematizing his deployment of the ethical axis of good on evil, on which his
entire discussion of genre turns (*PU*, 110). In Propp's case, it means
problematizing his treatment of character (*PU*, 123). The *tour de force*
reading of *Wuthering Heights* Jameson offers in support of his re-reading
of Propp is equally revealing of his re-reading of Frye, although it
makes no direct reference to Frye, and can therefore stand duty as a
representative instance of what is meant overall by historicizing genre.
As we saw above, the ethical axis of good on evil is susceptible to rewriting in the terms of Nietzsche's theory of *ressentiment* which, as Jameson
puts it, 'unmasks the concepts of ethics as the sedimented or fossilised
trace of the concrete praxis of situations of domination' and is therefore
to be rejected as a supreme form of 'false consciousness' (*PU*, 117).
Jameson inverts the Nietzschean formula and treats the ethical binary as
a symbolic solution to a set of concrete social problems. Thus, as he
says, what seems Byronic about Heathcliff might just as well be seen as
Nietzschean, the implication being that any inquiry into the good or
evil of Emily Brontë's brooding hero will be a lure, an ideological
distraction.

Applying Propp's insights we see that this is a lure in a second – one
imagines ideologically reinforcing of the first illusion – way: Heathcliff

is not the hero of *Wuthering Heights*. He is rather something Propp calls the donor, a category Jameson elsewhere argues (in *The Prison-House of Language*) is in fact the dramatic core of narrative (*PU*, 126; *SV*, 65–69). His role is to restore the fortunes of the Earnshaws and Lintons, the two families at the centre of this dynastic drama; but also to rejuvenate them, lift them out of their historical slumber. Heathcliff is in this regard the embodiment of history – he earns his wealth by leaving the Heights and going away, presumably to the colonies, and making his fortune and remaking himself into the bargain. But he isn't the hero because the central narrative line does not turn on his fate, but the fate of the two main families. Speculation about Heathcliff's ethical character should thus be seen as a rising to the surface of the cultural revolution his career embodies – his injection of capital earned abroad and (we assume) by merchant means betokens a beginning of the end of the pastoral existence hitherto enjoyed by the Earnshaws and Lintons. Our indictment of his ethical character is thus at the same time an indictment of the transition from the semi-feudalism of the Heights in pre-Heathcliff times to the nascent merchant-capitalism of Heathcliff's age.[22]

Notes

1 Jameson gives a long account of his response to New Historicism in *PCL*, 181–217.

2 The same image is used in *IT2*, 158.

3 J.-L. Lyotard, *The Postmodern Condition: A Report on Knowledge* (trans. G. Bennington and B. Massumi; Minneapolis: University of Minnesota Press, 1984) p. xxiv. Perry Anderson (*OP*, 29) argues that Lyotard only ever had one metanarrative in mind when he coined the term in 1977 and that was Marxism.

4 Lyotard, *Postmodern Condition*, 31–37.

5 C. West, 'Fredric Jameson's Marxist Hermeneutics' *Boundary 2* 11:1–2 (1982) p. 189.

6 J. Derrida, 'Marx & Sons' in M. Sprinker (ed.), *Ghostly Demarcations: A Symposium on Jacques Derrida's Spectres of Marx* (London: Verso, 1999) p. 246.

7 Novelist Alison Lurie has offered an exquisitely 'historicized' counter-reading of *Narnia* which sees Aslan as the symbol of Britishness (think of the lions at the base of Nelson's column in Trafalgar Square) and the series as a whole as an allegory for the decline of the British Empire. A. Lurie, 'The Passion of C.S. Lewis', *The New York Review of Books*, LIII:2 (2006) pp. 10–13

8 Nature is itself a codeword – it simply stands for (and usefully estranges our conception of) the exigencies of the present.

9 See, in particular, the discussion of Norman Holland and Claude Lévi-Strauss (*SV*, 25).

10 C. Lévi-Strauss, *Tristes Tropiques* (trans. J. and D. Weightman; London: Penguin Books, 1992) p. 197.

11 P. Biskind, *Easy Riders, Raging Bulls: How the Sex 'n' Drugs 'n' Rock 'n' Roll Generation Saved Hollywood* (London: Bloomsbury, 1999) pp. 263–68.

12 Žižek's (*TN*, 149) claim that the fascinating presence of the shark serves to block our inquiry into the social is in this respect off-target. What Jameson is suggesting is in fact the very opposite: the emptiness of the shark as symbolic vehicle encourages a reading of the text that highlights its social content all the better to contain it. Rather than block our inquiries, the shark solicits and absorbs them. For a more detailed discussion of Žižek's reading of *Jaws* see R. Butler, *Slavoj Žižek: Live Theory* (New York and London: Continuum, 2005) pp. 44–47.

13 On a related note, Jameson (*GAH*) reads James Dickey's novel *Deliverance* and the John Boorman film based on it (another example of 'New Hollywood') in a similar manner, as an attempt to erase the cultural legacy of the 'New Deal'.

14 C. Belsey, *Critical Practice* (London: Routledge, 1980) p. 129.

15 The phrasing here is deliberate – 'respect for elders' is a phrase George W. Bush likes to use in speaking of the 'values' he learned in the course of his own childhood.

16 Questions of this type were brought to our attention by Michel Foucault under the rubric of 'bio-power'.

17 S. Greenblatt, 'Who Killed Christopher Marlowe', *The New York Review of Books* LIII:6 (2006) p. 44.

18 N. Klein, *No Logo* (London: Flamingo, 2000) p. 237.

19 Walter Benjamin's 1927 essay on his visit to Moscow captures with typical acuity and brevity the existential nature of cultural revolutions: It is life lived 'as on a laboratory table. And as if it were a metal from which an unknown substance is by every means to be extracted, it must endure experimentation to the point of exhaustion. No organism, no organisation, can escape this process' (W. Benjamin, *One-Way Street* [trans. E. Jephcott and K. Shorter; London: Verso, 1979] p. 186).

20 G. Deleuze and F. Guattari, *A Thousand Plateaus* (trans. B. Massumi; Minneapolis: University of Minnesota Press, 1987) p. 230.

21 N. Frye, *Anatomy of Criticism* (London: Penguin, 1957) p. 99.

22 It is worth noting here that in *Signatures of Visible* (228–29) Jameson offers the hypothesis that the transition from feudalism to capitalism is the fundamental Marxist narrative (on a par with, though much stronger than, Freud's Oedipal complex).

Chapter 4

Postmodernism

> It is only at this price – that of the simultaneous recognition of the ideological and Utopian functions of the artistic text – that a Marxist cultural study can hope to play its part in political praxis, which remains, of course, what Marxism is all about.
>
> Fredric Jameson, *The Political Unconscious*

Perry Anderson has, with his exquisite sense of occasion, canonized the first public reading of Jameson's essay 'Postmodernism and Consumer Society' at the Whitney Museum of Contemporary Art in the fall of 1982 as a foundational moment for critical and cultural theory that can justly be compared to Derrida's equally famous first reading of 'Structure, Sign, and Play in the Discourse of Human Sciences' at Johns Hopkins University in 1966 – the latter is generally said to have launched post-structuralism, while the former in Anderson's words 'redrew the whole map of the postmodern at one stroke' (*OP*, 54).[1] This first version of the essay, which was to know a number of versions and eventually grow into a book of the same title, was subsequently published a year later in *The Anti-Aesthetic*, edited by Hal Foster, a book that quite unusually for a compilation of essays (even for one containing such a constellation of intellectual luminaries as this – Jean Baudrillard, Kenneth Frampton, Jürgen Habermas, Fredric Jameson and Edward Said to name only a few) had enormous influence, signalling for many the start of a whole new period in critical thinking.[2] A fuller version of the essay was subsequently published in *New Left Review* in the spring of 1984 under the new title of 'Postmodernism, or, the Cultural Logic of Late Capitalism'. The definitive version appeared in 1991 as the program essay of the book of the same title.

Few essays have had the literally global impact of 'Postmodernism, or, the Cultural Logic of Late Capitalism'. Even fewer can claim to have changed the way the world thinks about itself. Yet that is precisely what it did. For the next decade or so, until the concept of globalization finally supplanted it as the new zeitgeist term, 'postmodernism' functioned as the essential conceptual anchor for virtually every critical discussion in both academic and non-academic circles about 'the way things are now'. Jameson did not invent the term 'postmodernism' – neither did its other claimant, Jean-François Lyotard – but in his hands it became a concept in which the lines of flight (to use Deleuze and Guattari's useful notion) connecting contemporaneous, but nonetheless non-synchronous and disparate cultural effects, suddenly became visible.

Although this essay appears in retrospect to have had the sudden and brilliantly illuminating effect of 'magnesium flares in a night sky' (to use Perry Anderson's vivid phrase), its genesis was anything but sudden. As is obvious from the brief publishing history given already, Jameson spent nearly a decade just on this one essay. If one sees this essay, as one should, as simply the leading edge of a larger project, then one can trace its origins back at least another decade. As early as 1971, in *Marxism and Form*, Jameson began identifying and classifying the symptoms of the age he would later term the postmodern, but then simply termed 'new modernism' (*MF*, 413). There he observes that 'the development of the postindustrial monopoly economy capitalism has brought with it an increasing occultation of the class struggle through techniques of mystification practised by the media and particularly by advertising in its enormous expansion since the onset of the Cold War'. What this means, in 'existential terms', he continues 'is that our experience is no longer whole: we are no longer able to make any felt connection between the concerns of private life, as it follows its own course within the walls and confines of the affluent society, and the structural projections of the system in the outside world, in the form of neo-colonialism, oppression, counterinsurgency warfare' (*MF*, xvii–xviii). The full pungency and indeed pugnacity of this last phrase becomes apparent when it is recalled that it was written at the height of the Vietnam War, when the nightly news bulletins were a constant, grisly reminder of the human cost of ideological differences. As Jameson will say two decades later in the introduction to *Postmodernism, or, the Cultural Logic of Late Capitalism*, 'postmodern culture is the internal and superstructural expression of a whole new wave of American military and economic domination throughout the world: in this sense, as throughout class history, the underside of culture is blood, torture, death, and terror' (*PCL*, 5). And on the domestic front, it is a substitute and compensation for the failed radical movements of the 1960s which despite the huge cultural transformations they brought about left all the basic power structures intact (*PCL*, xvi).

It will be recalled, too, that in the opening pages of *The Political Unconscious*, published in 1981, Jameson explicitly situates his inquiries into the social-symbolic function of narrative in an historical framework that we now have no difficulty in recognising as postmodern. Our readings of the past, he writes, 'are vitally dependent on our experience of the present, and in particular on the structural peculiarities of what is sometimes called the *société de consummation* (or the "disaccumulative" moment of late monopoly or consumer or multinational capitalism), what Guy Debord calls the society of the image or of the spectacle'. The point of this necessary labour of situating one's reading of the past in a rigorous account of the present, he continues, is that 'in such a society, saturated with messages and with "aesthetic" experiences of all kinds, the issues of an older philosophical aesthetics themselves need to be historicised, and can be expected to be transformed beyond recognition in the process' (*PU*, 11). This quite trenchant statement about the differently structured nature of present-day society should not be mistaken for a typical ivory-tower jeremiad about the decline of reading as a cultural practice and the culturally obliterating rise of a deplorable 'digital culture' – a catch-all phrase that encompasses TV, film, email, the internet, i-pods and so forth. If it is a denunciation of anything, then it is a denunciation of a critical theory that has been too slow in changing to meet the challenges of a rapidly evolving historical situation and now finds itself unable to say anything critical about that situation which is not automatically anachronistic or, worse, accommodated by the market itself.[3] This is the challenge he sets himself in writing *Postmodernism* – how to continue to think and write historically and indeed critically in an era that has forgotten what historical and critical thinking means. His strategy is to try to outflank it by thinking about it in a systemic and abstract way.

Postmodern period

Andy Warhol and pop art, but also photorealism, and beyond it, the 'new expressionism'; the moment, in music, of John Cage, but also the synthesis of classical and 'popular' styles found in composers like Phil Glass and Terry Riley, and also punk and new wave rock (like the Beatles and the Stones now standing as the high-modernist moment of that more recent and rapidly evolving tradition); in film, Godard, post-Godard, and experimental cinema and video, but also a whole new type of commercial film . . . Burroughs, Pynchon, or Ishmael Reed, on the one hand, and the French *nouveau roman* and its succession, on the other, along with alarming new kinds of literary criticism based on some new aesthetic of textuality or *écriture*. (*PCL*, 1–2)

What *Postmodernism* charts is the long and slow coming into being, and our perhaps even longer and slower coming to consciousness, of the new 'cultural dominant' (this concept will be discussed in more detail in the next section) henceforth known as postmodernism.

> In periodising a phenomenon of this kind, we have to complicate the model with all kinds of supplementary epicycles. It is necessary to distinguish between the gradual setting in place of the various (often unrelated) preconditions for the new structure and the 'moment' (not exactly chronological) when they all jell and combine into a functional system. This moment is itself less a matter of chronology than it is of a well-nigh Freudian *Nachträglichkeit*, or retroactivity: people become aware of the dynamics of some new system, in which they are themselves seized, only later on and gradually. (*PCL*, xix)

The period we now know as the postmodern began in the early 1970s. Architectural historian Charles Jencks, often credited with giving the term 'postmodern' its present sense, dates the advent of this period rather more precisely (*OP*, 21–23). It began, he famously says, at 3.32pm on 15 July 1972, with the demolition of the Pruitt-Igoe housing project in St Louis.[4] This moment is chosen because, according to Jencks at least, it signalled a radical shift of consciousness – gone was the essentially modernist idea which we associate with such incandescent figures as Le Corbusier that architecture could or indeed should be used to improve peoples' lives, not just materially, but socially and culturally as well. The ideals that had once inspired such utopian programs for urban transformation as Le Corbusier's 'Radiant City' and Ebenezer Howard's 'Garden City' were for all intents and purposes declared dead. From now on, pragmatism and market-savvy would hold sway.[5] The chief ideologues and architects of this latter position were the authors of *Learning from Las Vegas*, Robert Venturi, Denise Scott Brown and Steven Izenour, who described buildings of the type detonated in St Louis as 'ducks' (by which they meant any building which aspired to an overall symbolic form) and advocated in their stead something they called the 'decorated shed' (which subordinates form to function and only afterwards applies ornament).[6] Jameson acknowledges the importance of Jencks' work in describing the first signs and symptoms of this new thing and giving it a name, but treats his propositions as the partially worked-out bases for creating a new problematic rather than a set of received facts (*PCL*, 419 n. 2). If it is true that a seismic change of consciousness occurred on that fateful afternoon in July 1972, then what were the conditions of possibility underwriting that change? What was the nature of the cultural revolution that must have taken place for this 'truth event' (to use Badiou's notion) to have occurred? In short, if postmodernism did herald a change in cultural sensibility it cannot only have been a matter of varying architectural style and cultural taste, although that is how it was first characterized.

But if the architecture historians like Jencks do not take things far enough in their account of the advent of the postmodern by restricting their investigations to matters of style (even as they make pronouncements of a social and cultural order), then sociologists like Daniel Bell, whose slogan 'post-industrial society' was a precursor to postmodernism, take things too far by declaring that there has been an historic rupture or break and that the postmodern spells a whole new era as different from the modern as the Enlightenment was from the Dark Ages. Such a thesis requires that we accept the view that capitalism has somehow come to an end (albeit without becoming something else). An early enthusiast of the kind of technology led capitalism that figures as diverse in their political sympathies as Ronald Reagan and Bill Clinton would later celebrate under the innocuous-sounding rubric of the 'New Economy', which holds that all the old impediments (i.e., the rising cost of labour) to the continuous growth of productivity can be overcome by technological innovation (i.e., computers), Bell is something of a *bête noir* for Jameson.[7] As an enormously influential apologist for the status quo, he stands for the unpalatable idea that capitalism 'won' – the apparently commonsense thesis that not only did capitalism somehow manage to resolve all its social and cultural contradictions and deliver a society as good as can be wished for, it also triumphed over all the alternative systems and extinguished the need for ideology. Francis Fukuyama's 1992 *The End of History and the Last Man*, based on his 1989 article 'The End of History', which seized upon the falling of the Berlin Wall as the occasion for an epoch-making claim, is the apotheosis of this viewpoint, which in the name of Hegel consigns Marx to the dustbin of history for the twin failing of not having foreseen how good capitalism could be and how bad communism would be. While he is quite willing to acknowledge that on the surface things have changed a great deal, Jameson is utterly unwilling to concede that these changes mean there has been a rupture, much less an Hegelian *Aufhebung*, of the kind Bell and Fukuyama wax so evangelical (*CT*, 88–92). Capitalism has neither triumphed nor magically transformed itself into some perfect social system that leaves nothing else to be desired.

What has happened, rather, is that capitalism has expanded past its previous limits, penetrating and subsuming all the remaining enclaves. It has entered a 'Third Age', as the Marxist historian Ernest Mandel termed it in his path-breaking book *Late Capitalism*, which (as Jameson readily acknowledges) provides the template for Jameson's account of postmodernism.[8] But as several critics have noticed, Jameson does not stick to the script exactly, indeed he makes several adjustments of his own, the most consequential of these having to do with the dating of the commencement of this new period.[9] Postmodernism is, Jameson argues, the cultural logic of late capitalism, but its constitutive features – with certain isolated exceptions – didn't become visible until the 1970s, some thirty years into the 'Third Age' which for Mandel essentially begins in the aftermath of World War II when global capitalism had to face down the twin challenges of post-war reconstruction and rapid and wide-spread decolonization. The reason for this lag is quite straightforward – cultural change is not in lockstep with economic change, it takes time for the effects of the latter to be registered in the outputs of the former. By the same token, cultural change can race ahead of economic change, anticipating its effects long before they've been realised (*ST*, 76).

Late capitalism took off in the post-war period with a stunning two decades of high prosperity in First World countries, spurred by the twin engines of consistent sector-wide economic growth and rising individual incomes (which in turn promoted unprecedented levels of personal spending, effectively creating 'consumer culture'). The 1950s and the early 1960s are for this reason generally looked back on with consider-able nostalgia and no more so than from the vantage point of the 1970s when everything seemed to be going awry (Jameson mentions George Lucas's *American Graffiti* [1973] and Francis Ford Coppola's *Rumble Fish* [1983] as the paradigmatic early examples of this veneration of the 1950s). It is only in the 1970s that the economic contradictions of this new age of capital finally made themselves felt. The massive expansion of the productive capacity of the three economic superpowers of the era, the USA, Germany and Japan, finally exceeded the capacity of the market to absorb their output and after nearly two decades of astonish-ingly high levels of growth fell into a profound slump. The exuberance of the previous two decades suddenly felt like so much hubris.

Historical antecedents

Nowhere was this felt more severely than in the USA, which had also to absorb the virtually bankrupting expense of the Vietnam War it had waged unsuccessfully for the better half of the 1960s and the first few years of the 1970s. The USA's twofold response to the emptying of its treasury vaults was to (a) relinquish the 'gold standard' and float its dollar (or rather allow it to sink in value and effectively drag its competitors down with it) and (b) use its influence over the OPEC nations to drive up the cost of oil. The second strategy, which came to be known globally as the 'oil shock', hurt the European and Japanese economies because of their dependency on Middle Eastern oil, but greatly enriched the OPEC nations who reinvested their surplus dollars into US banks (who in turn funnelled it into Third World 'development' projects, thereby creating the catastrophic debt that weighs like a nightmare on countries like Argentina and Mexico).[10]

At a grassroots level, i.e., at the petrol bowser and at the shopping mall, this strategy was experienced by ordinary Americans as impoverishing because gas now cost more than it used to, as did all imported goods which no longer enjoyed the umbrella protection of a strong greenback. On top of that wages were lower, jobs scarcer and economic growth slower. What ensued was a decade of 'stagflation' (a neologism expressing the economically undesirable combination of stagnant growth and high inflation), 'capital flight' (the relocation of manufacturing to low-wage sites in the 'developing nations'), 'de-industrialization' (the reorganization of the economy around the finance sector, entailing massive job losses in the blue-collar sector), 'white flight' (the movement of middle-class whites out of the inner cities into 'gated communities' in the suburbs, intensifying race and class divisions) and a generalized ransacking of all the economic props First World society had unthinkingly relied on until then. New threats to the domestic order like 'drugs' and 'illegal immigrants' were conjured up to distract the population from these structural transformations and to license an intensification of law and order. And of course in the background, like an irresistible ground bass, there was the ever present threat of a nuclear war with the Soviets. As Jameson shows in *The Geopolitical Aesthetic*, these 'sad passions' find expression in the wave of 'conspiracy' movies, from the fantastic, like *The Parallax View* (Pakula, 1974), to the factual, like *All the President's Men* (Pakula, 1976), which came into prominence in this tumultuous decade.

Jameson dates the start of postmodernism in this period because it is only then that its true nature stood revealed. But he has another reason for wanting to use 1972–74 as the jumping off point and that is to mark out for separate attention the era known as the 'sixties'. Jameson's essay on this topic, simply titled 'Periodizing the 60s', is explicitly inscribed as a pendant to his program piece on postmodernism and should thus be read alongside it. What this essay describes in more detail than he was able to go into in the companion piece is the global cultural revolution that paved the way to postmodernism, setting in place its distinctive 'cultural logic' by overturning and reconstructing previously existing habits of mind and body. The 'sixties' begin with the decolonization of British and French Africa.

> The independence of Ghana (1957), the agony of the Congo (Lumumba was murdered in January 1961), the independence of France's sub-Saharan colonies following the Gaullist referendum of 1959, finally the Algerian Revolution (which might plausibly mark our scheme here with its internal high point, the Battle of Algiers, in January–March 1957, as with its diplomatic resolution in 1962) – all of these signal the convulsive birth of what will come to be known as the 60s. (*IT2*, 180–181)

But far from opening-out onto a whole new era of freshly defined freedoms, decolonization, in all its forms – from the peaceful to the violent – tended to be followed by the invention of new forms of imperial domination, articulated largely through the less than benevolent agencies of the International Monetary Fund and the World Bank (*IT2*, 184). For this reason, as Jameson goes on to point out, to speak of these events only in terms of 'power' or 'politics' (as a generation of 'postcolonial' critics have) is to miss the fundamental part played by the economy. All of which is brought into focus by the 'Green Revolution', the great (but far from benign) transformation of Third World agriculture via the importation of First World techniques of crop specialization, First World fertilizers and pesticides, and First World machinery, which was supposed to liberate the Third World from the perpetual threat of famine. Achieved at the enormous cost of the destruction of local economies (not to mention local 'ways of living'),[11] the actual result was a massive increase in productivity of certain crop types, such as cotton and sugar, at the price not only of an increased dependency on the vagaries of the global market, but also decreased food security by reducing the amount of foodstuffs grown locally.[12]

Alongside the 'Green Revolution', which put paid to the enclave of nature, one has also to take into account the militarization of Latin

America following the Chilean coup of 1973; the Chinese Thermidor, 1966–69; the Cuban Revolution of 1959; the Palestinian liberation movement following the Israeli seizure of the West Bank and the Gaza Strip in 1967; the Vietnam War, 1965–73; and, nearer to home, the Civil Rights movement in the USA, the student movement of May 1968 in France and the 'Red Brigades' in Italy. What all these events attest to, in both a positive and negative way, is that the 'sixties' was a period of 'unbinding' – it saw a 'prodigious release of untheorized new forces: the ethnic forces of black and "minority", or Third World, movements everywhere, regionalisms, the development of new and militant bearers of "surplus consciousness" in the student and women's movements, as well as in a host of struggles of other kinds' (*IT2*, 208). It gave rise to the feeling, at once utopian and dystopian, that anything – including the most corrupt, most violent, most despicable practices – was possible, disenchantment with the political process being as much a feature of this period as the thought that participation in radical politics could lead to change. Insofar as any of these events registered in the political unconscious of the First World we have a greatly enlarged global media to thank. If the 'Green Revolution' put paid to the enclave of nature, it was the advent of television that ultimately plundered the enclave of the unconscious. 'If there is any single technological watershed of the post-modern, it lies here. If we compare the setting it has created to the opening of the century, the difference can be put quite simply. Once in jubilation or alarm, modernism was seized by images of machinery; now, postmodernism was sway to a machinery of images' (*OP*, 88). Television colonizes our attention, our very consciousness, and *derealizes* (Sartre's word) the world into the bargain. Television has had two principal historical effects: (1) it gives us the image of the thing and promotes the illusion that the image is a satisfactory substitute for the thing – this is the essential meaning of Debord's remarkable formula that the final form of the commodity is the image; (2) it synchronizes the non-synchronous (it is by definition always in at least two places at once – the site of its broadcast and the site of its reception) and brings the whole world into the realm of the immediate (one no longer has to wait for news to come in, as in some nineteenth-century realist novel).[13]

What Jameson is reaching for here, with the aid of Mandel, is something he calls a 'unified field theory' of the 1960s: what he shows is that technology is an instrument of social transformation in both the First World (computerization) and the Third World (mechanization) and that the peasant revolutions in the Third World are functionally equivalent to the student and worker revolts in the First World (in both cases they sprang from a disequilibrium between the changing economic conditions and the still reactionary cultural conditions). Late capitalism can only be properly understood, then, as the setting in place of both the new economic conditions we now habitually refer to as 'globalization' and the appropriately readjusted mental habits to go with it. As such, 'the "postmodern" is to be seen as the production of postmodern people capable of functioning in a very peculiar socioeconomic world indeed, one whose structure and objective features and requirements . . . would constitute the situation to which "postmodernism" is a response' (*PCL*, xv). If we were to apply the methods of the metacommentary (see Chapters 1 and 3), then it should be clear that this peculiar socioeconomic world – which I have tried to describe above – is the history we should use as master text to decode the allegory of postmodernism. The picture that results should demonstrate how postmodern cultural texts coordinate 'new forms of practice and social and mental habits' with 'the new forms of economic production and organisation' that have been brought into being by the latest modification of capitalism (*PCL*, xiv). This is what Jameson does for us in his essay on the 'sixties', which by circumscribing a segment of history and trying to produce its concept, creates the conditions for a renewed intelligibility of the text as a response to a problematic situation.

Cultural dominant

'One of the concerns frequently aroused by periodising hypotheses is that these tend to obliterate difference and to project an idea of the historical period as massive homogeneity', but, Jameson argues, this is precisely why postmodernism should be grasped as 'cultural dominant' rather than a style: it is 'a conception which allows for the presence and coexistence of a range of very different, yet subordinate, features' (*PCL*, 4; *SV*, 203). Far from obliterating local difference, as many have claimed, the concept of the 'cultural dominant' rescues local difference; it gives it a place which is not that of sheer or schizophrenic difference. How does this work? In saying postmodernism is the new cultural dominant, Jameson is effectively saying it is the dominant cultural form of our age. As such, what it does is precisely what form does at every level, it manages heterogeneity – there is no better illustration of this than the form of the novel itself, which coordinates not only the interrelated narratives of several characters at once, occasionally also interpolating their private thoughts, but several different timescales as well, from that of the immediate event to the long durée of history itself. As an issue of form rather than content, the concept of the 'cultural dominant' points us toward the third horizon of the tripartite interpretative scheme Jameson proposed in *The Political Unconscious* and reprises here, namely that of cultural revolution or mode of production. As Jameson explained in *The Political Unconscious*, his original purpose in elaborating this horizon was precisely to invert the concerns of the previous two horizons (the symbolic act and the ideologeme, respectively) and focus on form rather than content, but in such a way that it is grasped as a form of content in its own right (*PU*, 99). The attempt to produce the concept of 'postmodernism' as a new 'cultural dominant' is explicitly inscribed by Jameson as an attempt to think through and describe the cultural revolution of our own period in history (*PCL*, xiv).

By doing so he aims to convert what had hitherto been used as a label for a certain kind of new style that had lately emerged in architecture, but also knew or seemed to share an affinity with stylistic developments in film, literature and the visual arts, into an explanation of those developments. In this way, what was previously considered form is now apprehended as content; the problem of form, meanwhile, is displaced to a higher plane. In *The Political Unconscious* Jameson suggests that genre offers the simplest and most accessible demonstration of this process inasmuch as it serves as a proving ground for the dominant anxieties and ideals of an age. This, at any rate, was true for the periods we now look back on as realism and modernism, as Jameson amply demonstrates in *The Political Unconscious*. But by the time we come to what he terms full-blown or high postmodernism, no single genre is capable of registering the historical situation on its own, and genre as a category loses a great deal of its usefulness. Partly this is because the historical situation is vastly more complicated in Ridley Scott's time than it was in Walter Scott's, but mostly it is because genres have become much more restrictive, their codes much more rigidly defined and policed. For instance, *Blade Runner* (Scott, 1982) is a neo-noir *policier*, regardless of its 'official' science-fiction content – all the key episodes in the film are textbook re-makes of 1940s genre films (the streetside diner at the start, the meeting with the evil genius and his female assistant, the chase scenes through a shadowy downtown, etc.); the science-fiction content lives on then as an 'idea' or molarizing force (to use Jameson's adaptation of Deleuze and Guattari) unifying and pulling together the essentially molecularized episodes of the story.[14] In postmodernism the task of representing the historical situation as a whole falls to the genre-system itself, which means as critics we have to read all the genres at once and try to see how in combination they seem to work together to produce the whole. The genre-system saves the critical usefulness of genre, but at the price of raising it to a higher or meta-level (*SV*, 175–77).

The concept of the 'cultural dominant' (together with its cognate 'totalization') has occasioned a great deal of misunderstanding. Simon During's 1987 essay, 'Postmodernism or Post-Colonialism Today', can be taken as emblematic.[15] It was one of the first to issue what is now the paradigmatic complaint that the world is not as fully postmodern as Jameson supposes it to be. Invariably some clichéd vision of the Third World as an isolated backwater unaware of global *realpolitik* is wheeled out as proof of this particular point. But whether or not everybody has heard of postmodernism or knows what it means is beside the point – postmodernism does not require universal recognition to be operative as a concept anymore than does, say, the concept of the world itself. Its validity derives from the analytic power of the conversations and discussions it enables rather than some documented empirical proof of its pervasiveness. Postmodernism is a 'force field' 'in which very different kinds of cultural impulses – what Raymond Williams has usefully termed "residual" and "emergent" forms of cultural production – must make their way' (*PCL*, 6). The equally paradigmatic counter-claim that there is more than one kind of postmodernism is in reality a sub-species of the previous complaint, inflecting it in such a way as to challenge the 'power' and the 'authority' of the supposedly dominant form. As Jameson readily acknowledges, he is very far from thinking all cultural production fits the criteria he elaborates for postmodernism, but to make the leap from there to the conclusion that there is no *one* form of postmodernism, only an endless series of postmodernisms, is to 'fall back into the view of present history as sheer heterogeneity, random difference, a coexistence of a host of different forces whose effectivity is undecidable' (*PCL*, 6). And in that moment the notion loses all explanatory power.

Symptoms of the postmodern

Jameson isolates five principal symptoms of postmodernity:

1. A new 'depthlessness' of the image ('waning of affect').
2. A weakening of historicity (pastiche).
3. A whole new type of emotional ground tone ('hysterical sublime').
4. A new relation to technology (geopolitical aesthetic).
5. A mutation in built space (cognitive mapping).

All of these symptoms are in their own quite different and often highly original ways responses to the historical situation mapped out in the foregoing. None of these symptoms can be thought in isolation from either 'late capitalism' (base) or each other (superstructure), however the connections that Jameson makes between them are not predetermined by this structure. By calling these features 'symptoms' I have pointed up the strong and necessary pessimism that guided the whole diagnostic process, but this impression is unbalanced if it does not also register his profound sense of optimism. It may well be that following the Brechtian edict his work starts with the 'bad new things', but he is invariably able to perceive in them an awakening of the Utopian Spirit.

The new 'depthlessness' of the image is Jameson's shorthand for three separate, though obviously interrelated propositions, which can be enumerated as follows: first, the meaning of contemporary art can no longer be conjured by imaginatively reconstructing its symbolic depths – it is not just the case that critical theory (particularly its deconstructive tropes) has de-legitimated the surface/depth hermeneutic model, although that has undoubtedly happened, but postmodern works of art themselves have abandoned it, thus the very nature of content has changed; second, there has been a mutation in both the object-world and in the subject, everything is now conceived of as textual, including history which has, accordingly, lost its potency; and third, there has occurred something Jameson rather enigmatically calls a 'waning of affect'. Comparative readings of Vincent Van Gogh's 'A Pair of Boots' and Andy Warhol's 'Diamond Dust Shoes' are offered as our entrée into what will unfold as one of the greatest and most consequential reclassification and re-categorization of cultural works. Van Gogh's painting, if it is 'not to sink to the level of sheer decoration', a constant risk in our depthless age, 'requires us to reconstruct some initial situation out of which the finished work emerges' (*PCL*, 7).

Jameson's argument, the architecture of which is already familiar to us from our reading of *The Political Unconscious*, is that unless we reconstruct that situation it will be impossible for us to grasp Van Gogh's work as a symbolic act, it will then inevitably become just another image. If we concentrate on its raw materials – 'the whole object world of agricultural misery, of stark rural poverty, and the whole human world of backbreaking peasant toil, a world reduced to its most brutal and menaced, primitive and marginalised state' – we can go some way toward mentally reconstructing the situation of the work, Jameson suggests (*PCL*, 7). Colour in Van Gogh, which however dreary the reality it ostensibly depicts nonetheless seems to explode off the canvas, can then be read as a 'Utopian gesture, an act of compensation which ends up producing a whole new realm of the senses, or at least the supreme sense – sight, the visual, the eye – which it now reconstitutes for us as a semiautonomous space in its own right' (*PCL*, 7). On a more metaphysical plane, that of Heidegger, the artwork's situation can be conceived as a problematical confrontation between Earth and World, or the meaningless materiality of the body and the social order itself. Either way, what is at work in such hermeneutical readings as these, is a kind of 'clinical' (Deleuze's word) operation whereby the work 'is taken as a clue or a symptom for some vaster reality which replaces it as its ultimate truth' (*PCL*, 7).

This ultimate truth is constructed by the viewer. It is a phenomenological truth rather than an ontological or epistemological truth, which is to say it is the truth of my experience, the truth *I* experience, but not a universal truth. If Andy Warhol's 'Diamond Dust Shoes' appears not to yield any such truth, it is because it makes no place for the viewer, it does not hold out to them the 'open door' of a known or at least knowable life world. Instead of worn brown leather boots, caked in the mud of the fields, unlaced and flung against the wall to mark the end of a hard day of labour, their vital place in a lifecycle of peasant work immediately obvious to us, Warhol's work proffers 'a random collection of dead objects hanging together on the canvas like so many turnips, as shorn of their earlier life world as the pile of shoes left over from Auschwitz or the remainders and tokens of some incomprehensible and tragic fire in a packed dance hall' (*PCL*, 8). There is no obvious pathway for the viewer to follow to restore the situation of the work: we are left to guess not merely what they mean, but how they might be made to mean. This brings us to the second proposition, the transformation in the object-world and in the subject. Warhol's images mortify the eye, but not in a way that could call to mind the artistic staple of the phenomenology of death, which would require a certain empathy or even sympathy for a prior loss we are unable to imagine for this particular work. Put simply, even if they were a 'pile of shoes left over from Auschwitz' it is not as though *that* is a knowable life world, so any attempt on our part to reconstruct the situation from which the work arose would inevitably lead to nothing but directionless pathos (we feel sorrow, but not for anyone in particular, just a poor nameless Jew, which cannot but be felt as a rebuke). Jameson attributes this effect to the impact of photography and more especially the photographic negative on contemporary art. In Warhol's hands, these things are put to paradoxical use. Colour, always already contaminated by its complicity with commodification (something that Warhol who began his career as a commercial illustrator working on magazine spreads and shop-window displays knew all too well), is drained away 'to reveal the deathly black-and-white substratum of the photographic negative which subtends them' (*PCL*, 9).[16] If one cannot reconstruct the life world out of which the work arises, all is not lost because one can usually get a sense of the work's emotional ground tone, as Jameson calls it, by isolating one's own subjective response, or what is more commonly referred to as the work's affect. But even then Warhol forestalls us because it is not clear how one should feel about his images – they neither evoke nor provoke anxiety, but leave us frustrated, our thoughts fragmented into a disconnected swarm of intensities.

Brian Massumi's apostrophe – 'Fredric Jameson notwithstanding, belief has waned for many, but not affect'[17] – is symptomatic of how little understood 'waning of affect' is as a feature of postmodernism.[18] Largely owing to the influence of Gilles Deleuze, 'affect' is one of those terms whose critical stocks are riding high right now, making Jameson's claim appear either outdated (it was made in 1982, after all) or, in a less charitable light, simply counterintuitive and wrong. But this assumes that Jameson and Deleuze mean the same thing when they use the term affect, which is not the case, although one may be forgiven for not noticing the difference between the two straightaway. Both Jameson and Deleuze trace the origins of the concept of affect back to high modernist sources – Van Gogh and Munch for Jameson and Kandinsky and Klee for Deleuze – but there the resemblance ends. To be sure, Jameson's analysis of the way the lurid orange, red and blue swirls in Munch's 'The Scream' (one of high modernism's most iconic and widely recognized achievements) enable the 'absent scream' to return 'in a dialectic of loops and spirals' in which 'sonorous vibration becomes ultimately visible, as on the surface of a sheet of water, in an infinite regress which fans out from the sufferer to become the very geography of a universe in which pain itself now speaks' is practically a textbook illustration of what Deleuze means by affect (*PCL*, 14). The difference is that for Jameson this vivid synaesthetic transformation of the anguished sound of pain into pained whorls of paint is to be read as the outward expression of an inner feeling, or more precisely the 'visible world' is nothing other than the inner 'wall of the monad on which this "scream running through nature" (Munch's words) is recorded and transcribed' (*PCL*, 14).

The surface of Munch's painting is, in other words, only intelligible when read against the backgrounded of a hidden depth, that of the ego or the monad whose 'wordless pain' is 'projected out and externalised' by the artwork 'as gesture or cry, as desperate communication and the outward dramatisation of inward feeling' (*PCL*, 11–12). As Jameson goes onto argue, this conception of hermeneutics and, more especially, this conception of subjectivity have been systematically repudiated by postmodern 'theoretical discourse' (*PCL*, 12–14). In this sense, one could plausibly argue that Deleuze's concept of affect is a reaction to and consequence of Jameson's 'waning of affect', for it is precisely a de-subjectivized (i.e., schizophrenic) and indeed 'depthless' account of the concept that he offers.[19] What Jameson means by affect then is the emotion(s) of the individual subject, understood as a self-enclosed ego or monad.[20] It does not survive into postmodernity because its precondition does not – the subject was one of the first casualties of theory's assault on the received ideas of modernity.

Jameson's 'waning of affect' hypothesis is then, as one would expect, ultimately historicizing in intent and surprisingly elegiac in tone: it is the pathologies of the ego, such as anxiety and alienation, but also hysteria, which have lost their relevance in the postmodern world. It is their 'affect' that has waned (in this respect, the persistence of such themes in the work of people like Slavoj Žižek is, strictly speaking, anachronistic and the pleasure we take from it nostalgic). 'The great Warhol figures – Marilyn herself or Edie Sedgewick – the notorious cases of burnout and self-destruction of the ending of the 1960s, and the great dominant experiences of drugs and schizophrenia, would seem to have little enough in common . . . with the hysterics and neurotics of Freud's own day or with those canonical experiences of radical isolation and solitude, anomie, private revolt, Van Gogh-type madness, which dominated the period of high modernism' (*PCL*, 14).[21] This does not mean that affect no longer has a part to play in postmodernity, nor that postmodernity is somehow wiped clean of all such feelings, emotions and anxieties of these older types. But such feelings have been shattered, as the subject itself has, into countless free-floating and impersonal 'intensities'. To speak of the 'waning of affect' is to acknowledge that contemporary experience can no longer be registered and reflected back using such prefabricated vessels as 'anxiety' or 'alienation'. As Deleuze and Guattari predicted when they created the concept of the 'rhizome', the new problem of postmodernity is precisely how – in the absence of an ego – to think the relation between all these new intensities thrown up by postmodern experience. Jameson's answer is that we have been compelled to 'spatialize' them: 'the most striking emblem of this new mode of thinking relationships', he writes, 'can be found in the work of Nam June Paik, whose stacked or scattered television screens, positioned at intervals within lush vegetation, or winking down at us from a ceiling of strange new video stars' force the 'bewildered viewer' to 'do the impossible, namely, to see all the screens at once, in their radical and random difference' (*PCL*, 31). Hence his thesis, which we will return to below, that in postmodernity our tendency is to foreground categories of space rather than categories of time.

But if there is no individual subject, and no distinctive feelings, only intensities of an impersonal type, then there can be no such thing as style in the traditional (i.e., modernist) sense of a personal and unique mode of expression. 'The disappearance of the individual subject, along with its formal consequence, the increasing unavailability of the personal style, engender the well-nigh universal practice today of what may be called pastiche' (*PCL*, 16). Pastiche is the imitation of a peculiar or unique style, but in contrast to parody or satire it is an imitation without a purpose, save that of the (perhaps private) pleasure of reanimating a dead language. It is a somewhat dispirited practice, however, because it has stopped believing in the possibility of creating a thoroughly new artistic language. Creativity, it holds, is henceforth to be found in the ahistorical revival of lost, dead or dormant styles. The inaugural text of this type was Thomas Mann's *Doctor Faustus*, which deploys Adorno's delineation of the two pathways of modern musical experimentation, distinguishing between Schoenberg's planification, his austere and difficult formalism, and Stravinsky's exuberant eclecticism, as a means of working out the new status of the New. Ultimately, Mann decides in favour of Stravinsky, inasmuch as his text is an instance of pastiche, even if the official content of that text, the parts which deal directly with music (and for which Adorno provided technical advice), appear to uphold Schoenberg as modernism's approved keeper of the flame. The dialectical tension here between the symbolic level of the sentence production itself (Stravinsky's eclecticism) and the ideational level of the ideologeme (Schoenberg's planification) is symptomatic of the cultural revolution we call full-blown postmodernism, which proclaims itself free from all the 'old' constraints of aesthetics up to and including the most consequential of them all, namely the distinction between art and non-art, but also wants us to believe it has not thereby fallen into sheer decoration. It also explains a good deal of the hostility to this particular thesis which seems to be suggesting postmodern cultural production is somehow inauthentic, which in a sense it is, except that as Jameson points out this judgement (archetype of modernism that it is) is itself outmoded by postmodernism. This hostility, in its more affirmative iterations, has tried to recuperate and redeem pastiche under the nobler-sounding heading of irony, which is one of those concepts that, as Jameson puts it, enable us 'to have our cake both ways and deny what we affirm, while affirming what we deny' (*AF*, 177). In this way, irony enables us to evade any truth-telling of a determinate kind and for that reason Jameson sets it aside as politically compromised and compromising formulation.[22]

Pastiche is perfectly suited to what Jameson describes as an 'historically original consumers' appetite for a world transformed into sheer images of itself' (*PCL*, 18), or what is more generally known as the culture of the simulacra. The effect of this change has been to turn the past itself into an image, or rather a vast pile of images like the discarded photo album of some God-like creature. 'Yet it should not be thought that this process is accompanied by indifference: on the contrary, the remarkable current intensification of an addiction to the photographic image is itself a tangible symptom of an omnipresent, omnivorous, and well-nigh libidinal historicism' (*PCL*, 18).[23] Jameson offers three cases of this 'passionate attachment' (to use Butler's concept) to the past: neo-historicism in architecture, cinematic 'nostalgia for the present', and the new form of the historical novel. Jameson says very little about the first, save that it corresponds to the transition to the 'decorated shed' model of building championed by Robert Venturi, which in line with pastiche's effacement of the distinction between high and low culture cannibalizes rather than quotes the styles of the past. Since I will have more to say about architecture in the discussion of the final feature, the mutation in built space, I will reserve my remarks on this subject until then.

As for the second case study Jameson offers, it has to be said 'nostalgia for the present' is another one of those slogans like 'waning of affect' that takes a bit of getting used to. It does not mean to suggest we are nostalgic for our own present, which would be a category mistake, albeit an intriguing one since it would imply the complete loss of historicity of even that minimal schizophrenic variety; rather, it suggests we are nostalgic for the lost 'presentness' of the past. But not the past of that vivid and 'warm' kind Jameson evokes in *The Political Unconscious*, which finds its inspiration in history as an 'untranscendable horizon'. It is rather a glossy kind of past, like the one found in fashion shoots, conveyed via re-motivated symbols and objects of a particular period – clothing and hairstyles pre-eminently, but also technology, especially its conspicuous absence, and even body shapes and comportment (the eye-catching and much publicized 'presence' of female body hair in a recent made-for-TV version of *Sons and Lovers* [Whittaker, 2003] being an obvious, and obviously libidinally invested, example). But nostalgia films do not even necessarily have to be set in the past to achieve this particular effect – they can, and frequently do, reshape the present to look like an image of the past by editing out all signs and traces of our present. In this way both history and historicity are erased, leaving us with nothing but the brightly-lit nightmare of an eternal present.[24]

In the decade since Jameson's essay appeared, 'nostalgia for the present' films have continued to thrive. *Titanic* (Cameron, 1997), one of the highest-grossing films of all time, is a highly polished example of a nostalgia film, as is Peter Jackson's *King Kong* (2005). About both films one could no doubt say the same as has already been said about *Jaws*: the key issue is not what the equally outsized ship or gorilla stand for, but what ideological issues are they a pretext for 'working through'. In *King Kong* nostalgia is discernible on two levels: first there is the nostalgia for the 1930s period of its setting, but interwoven with that is a second-order nostalgia for other films – the original 1933 Schoedsack and Cooper version of *King Kong*, obviously, but also more recent films like *Jurassic Park* (Spielberg, 1993). No doubt Jackson was compelled to re-make *King Kong* in this way, rather than set it in the present as the 1976 John Guillermin version did, because recent events in New York, namely 9/11, make it impossible for a film so conspicuously invested in architecture (the finale requires a skyscraper) to avoid both the still-raw grief those events evoke, but also the egregious geopolitics that ensued. Had it been set post-9/11 the film could not have avoided treating the World Trade Centre as some kind of gigantic 'lack', in the Lacanian sense of the word, a rent in the city fabric calling for an intense engagement with the present.

The only other way of avoiding this would have been to set it in the future, inside the Daniel Libeskind designed 'Freedom Tower' that is to be built there. Such a strategy might have been able to yield one of the positive effects Jameson theorizes under the heading of 'Nostalgia for the Present', in a 1989 essay on Philip K. Dick's *Time out of Joint* that now appears as chapter 9 of *Postmodernism*: the perception of our present as the past of a determinate, albeit fantasized future, giving us a literal history of the present (*PCL*, 284; *AF*, 345). *King Kong* clearly fulfils the first two requirements of the 'nostalgia film' as Jameson defines it: it revives in fashion-plate form the New York of Schoedsack and Cooper's film, rather than New York itself; it avoids all contact with contemporaneity, up to and including that which we could not help but imagine. It also exhibits what Jameson notes are its key formal limitations. Because the whole 'effect' of the film presupposes the audience's recognition of a set of received historical stereotypes – from the look of cars, to the way men treated women[25] – its narrative is condemned to confirm those stereotypes (*CT*, 130). It figures this constraint, allegorically, by focusing the narrative on artists – the struggling actress, the love-sick screen-writer, the demented director, but also the Conrad-reading seaman – and by making it a story about the difficulty of making great art in a market economy.[26]

As for pastiche in literature, E.L. Doctorow's *Ragtime* is Jameson's key exhibit. Once again, pastiche is defined as a symptom of a deeper historical shift – if it is a negative judgement on Doctorow, which several critics (particularly Linda Hutcheon) have mistaken it to be, then it is only because it is a negative judgement on the times inasmuch as they seem to demand this kind of writing. What is culturally interesting about Doctorow's work, Jameson says, is the way it is marked by the cultural logic of late capitalism. Set in turn-of-the-century New York, the novel traces in epic fashion the complicated lives of three families which are representative of three distinct strata of New York society (Anglo-American establishment, marginal immigrant and semi-segregated black); its conceit – which is at the same time its marvellous innovation – is to treat fictional characters like real people and real people like fictional characters and essentially place all events on the same epistemological plane. As is the case with 'nostalgia film', the 'effect' this strategy generates presupposes a more or less clichéd understanding and recognition of the past, the kind one gleans from high school primers and 'official' histories, so it cannot deepen its vision of history without either losing its audience or seeming to turn into a comical counter-history (as when Xena teaches Hippocrates how to be a physician). Jameson reads this as an example of what historical novels look like after the loss of history as a vital referent. 'This historical novel can no longer set out to represent the historical past; it can only "represent" our ideas and stereotypes about the past (which thereby at once becomes "pop history"). Cultural production is thereby driven back inside a mental space which is no longer that of an old monadic subject but rather that of some degraded "objective spirit": it can no longer gaze directly on some putative real world, at some reconstruction of a past history which was once itself a present; rather, as in Plato's cave, it must trace our mental images of that past upon its confining walls' (*PCL*, 25). The only realism left to us is the realism of that experience of being locked inside a hyper-real world of simulacra. This development points, in turn, to other shifts in the organization and representation of time Jameson defines as the advent of a kind of schizophrenia (in Lacan's sense), whose essential experience is that of a profound disconnect between events and experiences.

In moving on to to the third feature of postmodernism, the presence of a new ground tone, we find that we are once again directed to think about the derisive effect of the commodification of both the past and our aesthetic response to it (this being the essential cause of the 'crisis of historicity' Jameson diagnoses). But now we are asked to look past the surface phenomena of pastiche and schizophrenic writing to what might be called the metaphysical dimension of postmodernism. For the past two centuries or more, all thoughts about human endeavour have used nature as their yardstick or 'other' against which both human capacity and human ambition are measured. For philosophers Burke and Kant, nature is the sublime, that object that always exceeds our categories (it is in Lyotard's terms the 'unpresentable'), while for historian Marx it is that which must be overcome in order satisfy basic wants. Nature has thus been revered and feared throughout history, but always as a kind of enemy. But since the Green Revolution, at least, this has changed quite dramatically – now, if anything, nature stands in need of rescuing. Climatic change is rampant, summers are hotter and drier, winters are colder, ocean levels are rising, the bio-mass of our seas is shrinking, forests are disappearing, and every couple of minutes another species of fauna vanishes for good. It is this conquered nature that Jameson has in mind when he offers the related bold proposition that culture is the new nature – today's entrepreneurs no longer look to the seas and the forests and the hidden minerals of the world in order to make their fortune, rather they look to culture itself: inventing a new computer application is more lucrative these days than finding a new gold deposit or oil reserve. Under such conditions, nature no longer commands the same metaphysical attention it used to. Imagine a God that needs our help to survive, instead of the other way around. Nature is no longer our other, our sublime. What has replaced it is technology, although not technology in and of itself (just as it was never a matter of nature in and of itself), but rather what technology stands for. With this new question and problematic we have arrived at the fourth feature of postmodernism.

But it is only the newer kinds of technology, those belonging to what is sometimes referred to as the 'Third Machine Age' or the 'Age of Information', essentially the silicon chip and its countless applications, which are able to evoke thoughts of this type, which Jameson suggests might be described as 'hysterical sublime'. The older types of machines, such as cars, trains and aeroplanes, which dominated the 'Second Machine Age', made humans equal with nature – it gave us unheard-of strength and speed (Superman is the supreme embodiment of this era, defined as he is by these twin characteristics of supernatural strength and speed). The machines themselves, steel-plated phallic emblems of congealed speed, had an imposing representational power our own feebler looking little plastic boxes and flickering monitors patently lack. We get no sense of what a computer can do, much less how it has been able to have a world-historical impact, simply by looking at it. Neither is it enough to simply depict them in use, as exhilarating as it was the first time Mulder used his cellphone to call Scully. 'Whether representation can draw directly, in some new way, on the distinctive technology of capitalism's third age, whose video- and computer-based furniture and object-world are markedly less graphic than the media and transportation technology of the second (not excluding telephones) remains one of the great open questions of postmodern culture generally' (*SV*, 15–16). Jameson's answer to this question is oblique. Our 'faulty representations of some immense communicational and computer network', for which the term 'technological sublime' is obviously apt (hysterical sublime is simply the same thing with the addition of the question: what does this computer want from me?), are, Jameson suggests, 'a distorted figuration of something even deeper, namely the whole world system of present-day multinational capitalism' (*PCL*, 37). The technology is mesmerizing because it provides a visible and readily recognizable 'representational shorthand for grasping a network of power and control even more difficult for our minds and imaginations to grasp: the whole decentred global network of the third stage of capital itself' (*PCL*, 38). Cinema is undoubtedly the medium that has best been able to grasp this potential of the new machines; but literature has also, in isolated cases (Pynchon is often singled out), been able to make much of it. Indeed, it was in William Gibson's 1984 novel *Neuromancer*, which launched the cyberpunk sub-genre, that cyberspace as we now think of it was first worked out in representational terms.

At length then we come to the fifth and final feature of postmodernism identified by Jameson, the mutation in built space. Jameson's principal exhibit is the Bonaventure Hotel in Los Angeles designed and built by John Portman in 1977. Owing entirely to this section of Jameson's essay, a truly bravura piece of architectural description it has to be said, this building has become – as Derek Gregory has rightly observed – one of the essential *topoi* of postmodernism.[27] It is the place where one can go to see the abstract rendered concrete, literally. Pilgrimages have been made there by Jean Baudrillard, Henri Lefebvre and Edward Soja, as well as dozens of other scholars, often to great disappointment – Jameson's writing exceeds the object in every direction, it is exhilarating and thought-provoking whereas the actual thing itself is rather dreary and undistinguished, just another 'non-place' (to use Augé's concept).[28] Featured in several films (the best of which are *Nick of Time* [Badham, 1995] and *Line of Fire* [Petersen, 1993]), as the hotel management proudly reminds all its visitors by placing brass plaques – one for each film, recording title, stars and director – on the wall at the entrance to the elevators, the Bonaventure is an icon of the *new* Los Angeles, whose epic poet, Mike Davis, was one of the first and fiercest respondents to this essay.[29]

From afar the Bonaventure looks like five grain silos, a large one in the middle and four smaller ones surrounding it on the outside, all bundled together and sheathed in a shiny black reflective skin, set atop a drab concrete box. Up close it is just another concrete and glass monolith whose features can scarcely be distinguished from any other office block. Jameson offers the Bonaventure as an instance of what has changed in the built environment of postmodernity, not – and this point needs to be stressed – as an instance, exemplary or otherwise, of postmodern architecture; indeed Jameson readily admits its design is uncharacteristic of postmodernism, if by that one means the work of a Robert Venturi, a Charles Moore or a Michael Graves. The Bonaventure is typical then of a widespread series of changes that have occurred in the built environment in the past thirty or so years, and any reading of this essay should be supplemented by a reading of several essays Jameson has since written on this expanded topic, particularly 'Culture and Finance Capital' (*CT*), 'The Brick and the Balloon' (*CT*), 'From Metaphor to Allegory' (FMA) and 'Future City' (*FC*), which deal with the issues of land speculation and the standardization of space in late capitalism, topics obviously germane to the subject at hand.

Jameson enumerates several features of the building that mark it out as new, but this litany is ultimately just preparation for, and the justification of, two interrelated propositions concerning the changed nature of not only built space, but the world itself. To begin with, the Bonaventure exhibits a new kind of logic of enclosure – strangely (one would think) for a hotel it does not open itself out towards the city, it has very few entranceways and they are curiously unmarked. Jameson reads this as an aspiration or desire to be a self-enclosed and self-complete 'mini city' and finds confirmation of his thesis in the reflective outer shell of the building which far from soliciting our gaze, as modernist monuments accustomed us to do, it seems rather to repel our gaze. When we try to gaze upon the hotel we see not the thing itself, but a distorted and fragmented reflection of the city around it, not to mention our own eye (think of that marvellous scene in the opening moments of *Blade Runner* [Scott, 1982] when the city is seen reflected in the iris of an eye). It is thus a placeless building, wilfully dissociated from its context. Inside this new 'self-complete' space, as Jameson calls it, the old categories of volume and volumes lose their meaning in the six-storey atrium into which elevators descend (the elevators travel on the outside of the building and only come inside at this point).

> You are in this hyperspace up to your eyes and your body; and if it seemed before that that suppression of depth I spoke of in postmodern painting or literature would necessarily be difficult to achieve in architecture itself, perhaps this bewildering immersion may now serve as the formal equivalent in the new medium. (*PCL*, 43)

This sense of bewilderment is exacerbated by the lobby itself which is both vast and unmarked – it is not clear, for instance, where one should check in. The result is confusion and disorientation. We thus arrive, abruptly enough, at the two key propositions whose existence we were alerted to above. The first is this: postmodern hyperspace 'has finally succeeded in transcending the capacities of the individual body to locate itself, to organise its immediate surroundings perceptually, and cognitively to map its position in a mappable external world' (*PCL*, 44). The second is this: the disjunction between us and the new forms of the built environment can stand as 'the symbol and analogon of that even sharper dilemma which is the incapacity of our minds, at least at present, to map the great global multinational and decentred communicational network in which we find ourselves caught as individual subjects' (*PCL*, 44).[30]

Although the sense of the second claim depends on our agreement with the first, ultimately it does not matter whether we personally find the Bonaventure as disorienting as Jameson did for us to understand his point, which is that it is the world itself, in all its postmodern complexity, that has exceeded our capacity to decide our place in it. 'Cognitive Mapping', a concept Jameson adapts from renowned urbanist Kevin Lynch's book *The Image of the City*, is the process of mapping individuals use to situate themselves (this concept will be discussed in more detail in Chapter 5). It is built up by walking around a city, dwelling in it, frequenting its haunts, and creating one's own 'field paths' through it: it therefore relies on icons and landmarks rather than map books and street signs, visual reference points rather than empirical data. Lynch's thesis, simple but powerful, is that cities rich in icons and landmarks are more 'liveable', because they are easier for us to 'cognitively map', while those cities – and he singles out Los Angeles as an example – poor in such things are more difficult for us to feel at home in. His message to future city planners, which continues to be heard, is that cities need monuments and iconic buildings in order that they may be lived in. We can therefore treat 'cognitive mapping', as Jameson in any case does himself in his later work, as primarily a problem of representation – how, given our limited representational means and limited representational technology, can we represent the world to ourselves in its fully globalized state? There is no definite answer to that question, although there are several noble attempts, and insofar as we lack an answer we are handicapped politically. If we cannot represent the world to ourselves how are we to understand it, much less change it?

Trajectories of the postmodern

Postmodernism did not begin at 3.32pm on 15 July 1972, but neither did it end (much less begin!)[31] at 8.46am on 11 September 2001, as many want to think. Postmodernism emerged slowly and unevenly in several different places around the world in the period following World War II and is still with us today. The term has lost a great deal of its currency in recent times, but none of its cogency. Yet the essential idea behind it lives on in the concept of globalization and we should not deceive ourselves that this terminological shifting of gears is ideologically innocent. But inasmuch as these changes can still only be identified as tendencies our analyses of it are, Jameson acknowledges, necessarily governed by the largely intuitive selection of what we think will persist or develop. 'All postmodernism theory is thus a telling of the future, with an imperfect deck' (*ST*, xiii). The better our ontologies of the present become, the more profoundly we feel the need for archaeologies of the future. 'What we really need is a wholesale displacement of the thematics of modernity by the desire called Utopia. We need to combine a Poundian mission to identify Utopian tendencies with a Benjaminian geography of their sources and a gauging of their pressure at what are now multiple sea levels' (*SM*, 215).

Notes

1 The analogy with Derrida is my own. Anderson's enthusiasm for Jameson's conceptualization of postmodernism comes as a surprise to anyone familiar with his earlier work. He once described its coinage as an attempt to cling to the wreckage of modernism (itself a futile and ideologically bankrupt term in Anderson's view), resulting in 'one void chasing another, in a serial regression of self-congratulatory chronology'. Originally written in 1983, it is not clear if Jameson's use of the term postmodernism is included in the remit of his critique. P. Anderson, *A Zone of Engagement* (London: Verso, 1992) p. 45.

2 This version of the essay is also reprinted in Jameson's *Cultural Turn.*

3 As for Jameson's own taste, he is quite explicit: 'I write as a relatively enthusiastic consumer of postmodernism, at least some parts of it: I like the architecture and a lot of the newer visual work, in particular the newer photography. The music is not bad to listen to, or the poetry to read; the novel is the weakest of the newer cultural areas and is considerably excelled by its narrative counterparts in film and video (at least the high literary novel is; subgeneric narratives, however, are very good, indeed, and in the Third World of course all this falls out very differently. Food and fashion have also improved greatly, as has the life world generally' (*PCL*, 298–99).

4 Coincidentally, these buildings were designed by the architect (Minoru Yamasaki) responsible for the twin towers of the World Trade Centre in New York.

5 D. Harvey, *The Condition of Postmodernity: An Enquiry into the Origins of Cultural Change* (Cambridge: Blackwell, 1990) p. 39.

6 R. Venturi, D. Scott Brown and S. Izenour, *Learning from Las Vegas: The Forgotten Symbolism of Architectural Form* (Cambridge Mass.: The MIT Press, 1972) p. 87.

7 For a critique of the 'New Economy' see D. Henwood, *After the New Economy* (New York: The New Press, 2003).

8 As Jameson noted in his foreword to Lyotard's *The Postmodern Condition*, Mandel provided an account of economic change that demonstrated that all the indices Bell drew upon to show that capitalism was over and done with could be 'accounted for in classical Marxist terms' (*F2*, xiv).

9 Perry Anderson (*OP*, 78–83) provides a useful account of critical responses to this particular discrepancy in Jameson's uptake of Mandel.

10 P. Gowan, *The Global Gamble: Washington's Faustian Bid for World Dominance* (London: Verso, 1999) p. 19–38.

11 The resulting loss of agricultural jobs initiated the huge migration of peasants in search of work to the cities, creating in their wake new urban wastelands. M. Davis, 'Planet of Slums: Urban Involution and the Informal Proletariat', *New Left Review 2* 26 (2004) pp. 5–34.

12 See Stephanie Black's astonishing documentary *Life and Debt* (2001) for a

contemporary example of the continuing impact of this so-called 'Green Revolution'.

13 The significance of this latter feature – the synchronizing of the non-synchronous – was brought to our attention by Benedict Anderson who traces its origins to the advent of the daily newspaper. B. Anderson, *Imagined Communities: Reflections on the Origins and Spread of Nationalism* (London: Verso, 1983).

14 Here I am adapting a hermeneutic model outlined by Jameson (*SV*, 208).

15 S. During, 'Postmodernism or Post-Colonialism Today', *Textual Practice*, 1:1 (1987) pp. 32–67.

16 Elsewhere, Jameson (*TL*, 199) suggests that exaggerated colouration can have a similar effect and should also be read as an expression of late capitalism.

17 B. Massumi, *Parables for the Virtual: Movement, Affect, Sensation* (Durham, NC: Duke University Press, 2002) p. 27.

18 In an interview with Anders Stephanson, Jameson responds to some of the critiques and confusions his argument has generated (*RP*).

19 Affect is the invention of a desubjectified literature according to Deleuze and Guattari. Therefore what they mean by affect can only take centre stage when what Jameson means by affect has in fact waned. See G. Deleuze and F. Guattari, *A Thousand Plateaus* (trans. B. Massumi; Minneapolis: University of Minnesota Press, 1987) p. 356.

20 In a later reconsideration of postmodernism, Jameson (*ET*, 709) offers a perhaps sharper account of what he means (although the notion of 'waning of affect' is not mentioned): postmodern life is no longer lived or thought in terms of destiny, as something that can find completion.

21 For an explicit development of this idea in relation to modernism see *IT2*, 14.

22 Irony, he argues, is 'the quintessential expression of late modernism and of the ideology of the modern as that was developed during the Cold War (whose traces and impasses it bears like a stigmata)' (*AF*, 179).

23 For an interesting development of the notion of 'libidinal historicism' (in the work of Flaubert) see *FLH*.

24 One has only to look at a MacDonald's store, or a Laura Ashley or Restoration Hardware furniture catalogue to see an example of this. It is instructive in this respect to compare *Maximum Overdrive* (King, 1986), a film directed by Stephen King based on one of his own stories, and the TV series *Dawson's Creek* – both were filmed in Wilmington, North Carolina, but they might just as well have been filmed on different planets so great is the contrast between their respective treatments of setting. Need I add that the ironic point of this comparison is that it is the Stephen King film which gives us the most 'realistic' representation of the contemporary 'dispersed' city.

25 Here the 'independence' of the female leads in both *Titanic* and *King Kong*, Kate Winslett and Naomi Watts respectively, is perhaps a symptom of this

constraint: it is a conscious anachronism, but one that is carefully contained – their characters may express 'feisty' opinions, but they do not actually do all that much except submit to the male gaze.

26 Jameson (*CT*, 133–35) describes this particular narrative turn as 'deplorable' because its 'pseudo-aestheticism' blocks even the most token kinds of historicity this mode of film can sometimes generate.

27 D. Gregory, *Geographical Imaginations* (Oxford: Blackwell, 1994) p. 139. Hal Foster has lately suggested that contemporary architecture, he is especially incensed by Frank Gehry, is now trying to live up to Jameson's description of what its space is like, producing in consequence bloated flights of fancy like the Guggenheim in Bilbao. H. Foster, *Design and Crime (And Other Diatribes)* (London: Verso, 2002) p. 38.

28 For a more developed discussion of this aspect of the critical response to Jameson's analyses of the Bonaventure see I. Buchanan, *Deleuzism: A Metacommentary* (Edinburgh: Edinburgh University Press, 2000) p. 144.

29 M. Davis, 'Urban Renaissance and the Spirit of Postmodernism', *New Left Review* 151 (1985) pp. 106–13.

30 The concept of the analogon is taken from J.-P. Sartre, *Psychology of Imagination* (London: Routledge, 1972). Jameson defines it as 'that structural nexus in our reading or viewing experience, in our operations of decoding or aesthetic reception, which can then do double duty and stand as the substitute and representative within the aesthetic object of a phenomenon on the outside which cannot in the very nature of things be "rendered" directly' (*SV*, 53).

31 B. Brown, 'The Dark Wood of Postmodernity (Space, Faith, Allegory), *PMLA*, 120:3 (2005) p. 734.

Chapter 5

Cognitive Mapping and Utopia

> Ontologies of the present demand archaeologies of the future, not forecasts of the past.
>
> Fredric Jameson, *A Singular Modernity*

Dialectical criticism's twofold purpose lies in uncovering the ways in which a now more or less fully global culture disguises its strategic interests while simultaneously keeping alive thoughts of the future. This task can be specified, in conclusion, as the urgent need to track down and diagnose two different kinds of failure of the imagination: the first is the failure to develop a usable representation of the present, one that enables us to see its limitations as well as its strengths, but more importantly enables us to perceive its deeply systemic nature; the second is a failure to imagine a form of the future that is neither a prolongation of the present nor its apocalyptic demise. For Jameson, this failure is even to be found in strong works such Deleuze and Guattari's, in which 'what looks like a critique of our social order and the conceptualisation of an alternative to it (in the *Anti-Oedipus*) turns out in reality to be the replication of one of its most fundamental tendencies. The Deleuzian notion of schizophrenia is therefore certainly a prophetic one but it is prophetic of tendencies latent within capitalism itself and not the stirrings of a radically different order capable of replacing it' (*ET*, 711).[1] These two diagnostic tasks are brought into focus via two concepts that each in their own way can be seen to draw a transverse line through Jameson's entire career: (1) cognitive mapping and (2) utopia. These two concepts should not be seen as either static or separate enterprises; they are at the core of Jameson's thought and practice as a critic.

Cognitive mapping

Colin MacCabe has rather perspicaciously said that cognitive mapping is 'the least articulated but also the most crucial of Jamesonian categories'.[2] It is certainly the case that its centrality as a concept is sometimes hard to see – it does not come into use until quite late, it then goes underground for several years, disappearing from view almost completely, and it is rarely even indexed when it is used. But lately it has re-emerged in such a way as to confirm the hypothesis that it really is at the core of Jameson's thought. It appears Jameson first used the term 'cognitive mapping' in a paper bearing simply that as its title at the landmark 'Marxism and the Interpretation of Culture' conference convened by Cary Nelson and Larry Grossberg at the University of Illinois at Urbana-Champaign in the summer of 1983 (*CM*). A version of that paper was subsequently published in the proceedings of the conference together with some extremely interesting questions and responses from the floor. This paper was then cut in two and subsumed into *Postmodernism*, where it appears as the final parts of the first and last chapters. The term makes a brief but crucial appearance in *The Geopolitical Aesthetic*, which was published in 1992 (but given as a series of lectures at the British Film Institute in London two years earlier in May 1990). After this, however, the term is rarely if ever used by Jameson except in interviews, and then only at the insistence of interviewers, for the next decade or so, until suddenly it reappears in his work on 'globalization' that, not uninterestingly for my purposes here, was developed alongside the magnum opus on utopia which we will examine in more detail in the next section. We might start by asking, then, what was cognitive mapping before it was cognitive mapping? And just as importantly, what happened to it in the 'lost decade'? If the concept really does span the full spectrum of Jameson's career, as I have asserted, then it must have had a life before it had a name, and if it continued to be significant even after its name stopped being used then it must have had several different names. Both of these answers are correct: cognitive mapping did have a life before it had a name and it has had several names since as well.

Its presentation in the form of a question in *Postmodernism* – how to map a totality – gives us an important clue as to the origins of this concept. Totality is a codeword in Jameson's work for 'class consciousness' and more allusively Lukács, to whom he attributes the concept (*IFJ*). As Jameson explains in his 1977 essay 'Class and Allegory in Contemporary Mass Culture', the precondition of 'class consciousness' is the visibility of a class to itself. 'This fundamental requirement we will call, now borrowing from Freud rather than Marx, the requirement of *figurability*, the need for social reality and everyday life to have developed to the point at which the underlying class structure becomes *representable* in tangible form.'[3] When Jameson uses the word 'totality', or speaks of 'totalizing' procedures, he means precisely this: no class or class fraction can function politically until it has found the means of representing itself to itself.[4] Strangely, as is obvious in the responses to Jameson's first presentation of the concept of cognitive mapping, the strongest objections to Jameson's advocacy of these terms have tended to come from within disciplinary areas such as feminism and race studies whose very *raison d'être* is to be found in the gap between existence and representation this concept presupposes.[5] For both feminism and race studies it is the control of representation by a more powerful other (the proverbial white Anglo-Saxon male) that creates the existential and political problems they theorize, which are usually described in terms of silenced, repressed or absent voices. Ironically enough, it is only by totalizing, that is, by projecting a totality greater than the surface appearance of things, that one can even begin to 'think' never mind hear and restore these lost voices. All the interesting interpretations these kinds of critical discourses have produced have tended to take the form of a demystification that discerns the presence of repressed people – whether by virtue of gender or race – in the manifest content of all the texts. By the same token, postmodern fiction's playful refusal of totalization celebrated by Hutcheon (among others), who detects this trait in writers as diverse in their political commitments as Rushdie, Grass and Márquez, should be historicized and its purposefully mystifying ideological strategy exposed.[6] Against this line of thinking, one might simply say a text that 'refuses' totalization should be treated with the same scepticism as an advertisement that 'playfully' claims not to be selling something.

The connection between cognitive mapping and figurability is made explicit by Jameson himself – as he told his audience at Urbana-Champaign: 'I tend to use the charged word "representation" in a different way than it has consistently been used in poststructuralist or post-Marxist theory: namely, as the synonym of some bad ideological and organic realism or mirage of realistic unification. For me "representation" is, rather, the synonym of "figuration" itself, irrespective of the latter's historical and ideological form' (*CM*, 348). Jameson's interest in figurability goes back to *Marxism and Form* (100–102). It is, moreover, the primary preoccupation of his literary criticism of the early 1970s, which interestingly enough focused almost exclusively on science fiction. One may hypothesize that he only stopped using this term when he saw how 'cognitive mapping' might be adapted to better suit his purposes. Such a hypothesis, regardless of its actual verifiability, has the merit of opening up the question of the difference between figurability and cognitive mapping, which ultimately has to do with the nature of the actual object they are trying to bring into view or find the means of representing. In the case of figuration the represented object is an abstract idea whose effect is to liberate us from the enslavement of the particular and the concrete.

> Thus in Whitman's catalogues, the individual finite items are released against the background of the general, indeed the universal, for which they stand. Thus in Surrealism there is at work a hermeneutic process in which Desire is identified behind all the individual and limited desires of an individual and associative system, in which Freedom is felt, instinct, behind the more limited and contingent freedoms of image and language. (*MF*, 102)

In effect, it is the difference between the transitive desire for this or that thing which, as psychoanalysis teaches us, can never be satisfied in any case since the real object will always pale beside its imagined or fantasized form, and some larger force of desiring unconstrained by a direct connection to a particular object which we might rather metaphysically term the desire for life itself (it being understood that in such a formulation, 'life' is no less a figuration than 'desire'). By contrast, the representational object of the cognitive map is an abstract concept whose effect is to render visible the various forces and flows that shape and constitute our world situation. To even speak of the 'world' is already to begin to produce a cognitive map because it is the articulation of a concrete 'totality' greater than what one can empirically verify. The very concept of the 'world', at its most mundane, amounts to the recognition and registration of a mysterious set of forces and effects that I cannot see, but nonetheless know have an influence over my existence.

Jameson's account of modernism suggests that the 'crisis' of figuration as a concept and the corresponding need for a replacement concept like 'cognitive mapping' occurred in the early part of the twentieth century; that is to say, the change in sensibilities or cultural revolution which betokens the need for the latter concept in latter-day critics such as ourselves occurred at the particular moment in history we now think of as the birthdate of modernism. Jameson stages this crisis in terms of modernism's coming to consciousness of the newly christened 'imperialism', a neologism that the great British historian Eric Hobsbawm informs us first became part of political and journalistic vocabulary in the 1890s (its first use dates back to the 1870s, but it was slow to take hold – it is not used by Marx, for example, who died in 1883), and thereafter became one of the central concerns of the age.[7] Imperialism is felt by Europeans in this era as a kind 'meaning-loss' (to use Jameson's own instructive term), because it requires that they take stock of the fact that 'a significant structural segment of the economic system as a whole is now located elsewhere, beyond the metropolis, outside of the daily life and existential experience of the home country, in colonies over the water whose own life experience and life world – very different from that of the imperial power – remains unknown and unimaginable for the subjects of the imperial power, whatever social class they may belong to' (*MI*, 11). Consequently, the subjects of the imperial power, or what we would now term the First World, cannot grasp – empirically, epistemologically, indeed existentially – the system that determines their lives 'as a whole'.

> Unlike the classical stage of national or market capitalism, then, pieces of the puzzle are missing; it can never be fully reconstructed; no enlargement of personal experience (in the knowledge of other social classes, for example), no intensity of self-examination (in the form of whatever social guilt), no scientific deductions on the basis of the internal evidence of First-World data, can ever be enough to include this radical otherness of colonial life, colonial suffering and exploitation, let alone structural connections between that and this, between absent space and daily life in the metropolis. (*MI*, 11–12)

The map (in the cartographic rather than cognitive sense) is not the solution, in other words, but the problem – the more one becomes aware of the existence of other worlds, of other lives, and more especially the intertwining of our lives with those nameless and faceless others, the less satisfactory the map seems as a representational device. And it is precisely imperialism as a form of commerce that journeys to the furthest reaches of the globe in search of new markets, cheap labour, raw materials and exotica, that 'stretches the roads out to infinity' thus rendering incomplete or lacking the old salvations of home and place (*MI*, 17). Place can only be restored as an idea, that is, rendered figuratively vital, at the price of coming to terms with imperialism and finding a way of neutralizing the 'meaning-loss' it induces. Modernism's answer to this, its famous inward turn and fascination with the inner self and the metropolis, not to mention its 'style', is incompletely understood if it is not seen in this light. Since 'representation, and cognitive mapping as such, is governed by an "intention towards totality" ', a term Jameson takes from Lukács, those limits to the imagination – infinite space, the infinite number of others – must be drawn back into the system and given a figurative form: 'a new spatial language, therefore – modernist "style" – now becomes the marker and the substitute (the "tenant-lieu", or place-holding, in Lacanian language) of the unrepresentable totality. With this a new kind of value emerges . . . for if "infinity" (and "imperialism") are bad or negative . . . its perception, as a bodily and poetic process, is no longer that, but rather a positive achievement and an enlargement of our sensorium: so that the beauty of the new figure seems oddly unrelated to the social and historical judgement which is its content' (*MI*, 18).

This thesis finds its confirmation in Irish literature from this period, which extends from the 1890s to the 1930s, because one finds there something like the coexistence of two modes of production – Dublin is at once an industrializing city, a centre of trade and commerce, and a colonized city, subject to foreign rule, and the focal point of a nationalist campaign for self-rule. As a modern city it desires to be its own master, but paradoxically mines its pre-modern past for the ideological resources it needs to galvanize the 'imagined community' of Ireland into action.[8] This is registered in the content of Joyce's work particularly, especially *Ulysses*, which is studded with peasant-like or village-like gossip, but also the ceaseless blandishments of commodities. But the crucial matter for Jameson is the way it is registered in the very form of the novel. 'The *Odyssey* serves as a *map*: it is indeed, on Joyce's reading of it, the one classical narrative whose closure is that of the map of a whole complete and equally closed region of the globe, as though somehow the very episodes themselves merged back into space, and the reading of them came to be indistinguishable from map-reading' (*MI*, 22). Confirmation might also be found in the literature of settler-nations like Australia and the USA, which in the same period were simultaneously obsessed with their relation to the 'mother country' (represented by the perseverance of out-of-date, and often climactically misguided customs), as the highly oedipalized figure of their past, and the 'frontier' (encapsulated in the body of the 'native'), as the highly romanticized concept of their future.[9] Modernism oscillates between figuration and cognitive map – we could even say it uses the one to obviate the other. It doesn't want to deal with or give recognition (in the strong Hegelian, 'master/slave' sense) to the nameless and faceless others in faraway dominion countries upon whose sweated labour it unthinkingly depends, so it conjures up figures of infinity to register the incompleteness of its picture of the world without having to explain it.

Metaphysics enables modernism to avoid history, but only for so long. As we saw in the previous chapter, the great harbinger of what we know today as postmodernism was the convulsive movements of decolonization that swept through Africa and Asia in the 1950s, releasing what Jameson terms 'an explosion of otherness unparalleled in human history' (*ET*, 709). The map never looked the same again after that. The 'blank spaces' Conrad's Marlow fantasized about in his childhood were all filled-in in a rush of change that left many in the West reeling. Science fiction, frequently literature's most sensitive instrument for detecting and registering change, captured some of the unsettling feelings decolonization provoked in the West with its nightmarish Malthusian tales of over-population, food shortages, perpetual wars, and so forth, for which the marvellous, reactionary, Charlton Heston vehicle *Soylent Green* (Fleischer, 1973) may stand as emblem (more critically, novels like P.K. Dick's *Martian Time-Slip* also managed to evoke colonialism's genocide of indigenous peoples). It is just such paranoid responses to this seismic change in the situation that renders such concepts as 'demography', a contender for the role assumed by 'cognitive mapping', unusable:

> [It] projects an immediate and subliminal image of the starving masses abroad and the homeless at home, of birth control and abortion. It thereby fixes the theme permanently at the political level and in a form which – all the more so because of its intrinsic urgency – does not move the viewer or the listener, the reader or 'public opinion' itself on to the underlying systemic reality, the root cause of missiles and permanent underemployment, or birth-rates abroad fully as much as break-ins at home. (*SV*, 2)

Demography is an example par excellence of an ideologeme (see Chapter 3) – it appears to be a problem in its own right, and its arguments similarly appear self-evident (it is apparently an inarguable truth that there are too many people on the planet), but to look at things this way is to ignore the deeper truth which Marxism insists on, namely that population would not be the problem that it is, or appears to be, if there was a more equitable distribution of wealth.

As George Monbiot has famously pointed out, today the world's richest five hundred people have more money than the world's poorest three billion. To represent this situation properly something more complex is required than the ultimately banal and unaffecting pathos of images of the starving. It is not because we privileged souls in the West are suffering from some spurious form of 'compassion fatigue', however, that makes this grim imagery so unaffecting. It is because such images are so many dead letters – we neither know their authors nor their addressees, they lack all causality. Only those representations which enable us to grapple with the deeper 'but nonvisual systemic' (*SV*, 2) cause of this misery will be duly affecting, and therefore deserving of the name of 'cognitive map'. By the same token, only those ameliorative strategies that aim to change the system itself can hope to make a difference (Bono teaming up with Bill Gates to provide assistance for AIDS sufferers in Africa may or may not help the millions of people with that disease, but either way it will do precisely nothing to change the global situation which leaves Africa stuck in the parlous developmental doldrums it finds itself in); and, I would add, only such utopian strategies will ever properly ignite our imagination. Compassion fatigue would be better termed a 'failure of the imagination' for what this numbness in the face of the intolerable suffering of others bespeaks is an inability to get a grip on the world situation today, as it really is. Cognitive maps are urgently needed to address this deficit. Examples are not lacking, but they are necessarily incomplete. Jameson singles out for special mention, the films *Dirty Pretty Things* (Frears, 2001), *In This World* (Winterbottom, 2003), the British TV series *Traffik* (Reid, 1989) and the documentary *Life and Debt* (Black, 2001), as works that have begun to discover the representational means of mapping the new space and more particularly the new form of sociality we call globalization (*RG*).

Utopia

For Jameson, coming to grips with 'how things are' is a necessary first step toward thinking about how things might be. Utopias stand on the shoulders of cognitive maps. Utopia, as desire and problematic, is never far from view in Jameson's work, indeed it is impossible to think of an example where it is absent, but it is usually confined to the conclusion (this is true of *Marxism and Form*, *The Political Unconscious* and *Postmodernism*). The exceptions to this particular rule of saving thoughts of utopia until last are: *The Seeds of Time* and *Archaeologies of the Future*. Postmodernism is the official topic of the first-mentioned work, which was originally conceived as a series of three lectures for the prestigious Wellek Library Lectures in Critical Theory hosted by the Critical Theory Institute at the University of California, Irvine in April 1991, but in reality it is about utopia. The official topic of the second-mentioned work, which appeared in 2005 after a gestation period of some 32 years, is, without a hint of dissemblance, utopia. *The Seeds of Time* cleared the way for *Archaeologies of the Future* by disenchaining utopia from dystopia, but more especially by showing that 'the most powerful arguments against Utopia are in reality Utopian' (*ST*, 54) themselves. These essentially formal and ideological arguments are supplemented by what one may designate an existential analysis of the anxiety, fear and indeed loathing felt in the face of utopia. Echoing the concluding chapter of *Postmodernism* Jameson insists in *The Seeds of Time* that there is 'no more pressing task for progressive people in the First World than tirelessly to analyse and diagnose' such feelings, which he suggests 'do not really spring from profound personal happiness and gratification or fulfilment in the present but serve merely to block the experience of present dissatisfaction in such a way that logically "satisfaction" is the only judgement that can be drawn by the puzzled observer from whom the deeper unconscious evidence has been withheld' (*ST*, 61–62). Freed from the necessity of this essentially negative task, the later book is then able to pursue its formal analysis of utopia in an affirmative manner.

Utopias differ from dystopias at the level of form and content: 'it is not merely that the pleasures of the nightmare – evil monks, gulags, police states – have little enough to do with the butterfly temperament of great Utopians like Fourier, who are probably not intent on pleasures at all but rather on some other form of gratification' (*ST*, 55). Beyond that, it has to be observed that dystopias generally have a narrative form, whereas utopias do not, lacking even the basic architecture of a subject-position around which to organize a narrative. Dystopias tend to be set in the 'near-future' and foretell disasters of all kinds, from old-fashioned Armageddon to twenty-first-century ecological catastrophe, e.g. *The Day After Tomorrow* (Emmerich, 2004). What is also noteworthy about the aforementioned film, whose director was responsible for that other block-buster dystopia of recent times *Independence Day* (1996), is the pivotal role of individuals, particularly climatologist Jack Hall (Dennis Quaid), who predicts the disaster and is the only one able to understand its first portents. Even if there is a utopian impulse to be detected here in the way in which one kind of society is destroyed in order to make way for another, here dramatized 'ironically' as an opening of the border between the USA and Mexico, the latter seen welcoming hordes of refugees from the USA and agreeing to give them sanctuary. A newly awakened consciousness on the part of the north of their fundamental dependency on the south is not in itself utopian, because, as is clear from the ending of the film anyway, the world-system is not changed by the sudden climate shift, power remains firmly in the hands of the USA and capitalism is as safe as ever. By contrast, then, 'the Utopian text does not tell a story at all; it describes a mechanism or even a kind of machine, it furnishes a blueprint rather than lingering upon the kinds of human relations that might be found in a Utopian condition or imagining the kinds of living we wish were available in some stable well-nigh permanent availability' (although he admits they can indulge in such flights of fancy, too) (*ST*, 56). Utopias are faced with a unique representational problem that the presence of narrative, which, because of its intrinsic demand for transformation (invariably figured by Hollywood as redemption), would only exacerbate: if we can imagine what the future might look like, then the suspicion arises that it is merely a repetition of the present, or else its prolongation, and not authentically new and different; by the same token, if the future looks appealing to us from our present vantage point how can we be sure it is not merely our wish-fulfilment, our own private fantasies writ large? (*ST*, 56; *AF*, 47).

'All authentic Utopias have obscurely felt this deeper figural difficulty and structural contradiction' (*ST*, 57) and have tended to respond to its demands by avoiding representations of utopian life and by concentrating on explicating the particular utopia's essential enabling mechanism. Sometimes it is literally a machine that then becomes the focal point of the text, its actual representational burden, but often it is an idea, or what we might term a 'social machine' – Ursula Le Guin's 1969 novel *Left Hand of Darkness* offers examples of both types. Set in circumstances that could easily be mistaken for a dystopia, the cold, perpetually frozen planet of Winter (thus calling to mind the staple of near-future dystopias, the nuclear winter), *Left Hand of Darkness* envisages a world in which everything that is problematic about sexual relations in contemporary society are absent. The inhabitants of Winter, the Gethenians do not have a permanently assigned gender, their bodies are essentially gender-neutral, or undecided as it might be better to say to avoid the misperception that they are somehow 'neutered' (which they are not!), except for certain 'seasons', cyclical periods of high sexual activity known as 'kemmer'. During this period gender emerges, but it is only a temporary assignment and varies from kemmer to kemmer so that one may be both female and male during the course of one's life. Far from being asexual, Gethenians are highly sexual, but in such a way that it feels or seems random and unmotivated to the outside observer. Indeed, one of the most troubling aspects of Gethenian physiology for the other-world emissary Mr Ai, is that Harth, his guide and companion, hitherto perfectly Platonic in his/her attitude towards him starts to lose that coolness as kemmer comes on, making for 'difficult' times between them as they try to renegotiate a new set of social protocols. Although its political point lies elsewhere, *Left Hand of Darkness* is libertarian inasmuch as it seems to be saying sex is only a problem because 'we' make it a problem – it is a problem between Ai and Harth because Ai sees it as an interruption of their friendship, whereas Harth regards it as a logical continuation of it.

True, the description of the kemmer houses is rather orgiastic, but it is equally clear that the real point of the novel is to expose the degree to which sex permeates every level of society, making it a political problem before it is a 'personal' problem. By contrast, the Gethenians see humans like Mr Ai as both oversexed and too-little sexed – to the Gethenian, humans are always in kemmer, but of a suspiciously low-grade variety that can be spread out over the whole year. *Left Hand of Darkness* is science fiction, rather than utopian, to the degree that its imagined solution to the social problem of gender relations is a fantastic one, relying on alien properties not available to us on earth, but its formal strategy of condensing all the sources of 'unfreedom' into a single scheme is perfectly consistent with the latter genre.

> Essentially, Gethenian physiology solves the problem of sex, and that is surely something no human being of our type has ever been able to do largely owing to the non-biological nature of human desire as opposed to 'natural' or instinctual animal need. Desire is permanently scandalous precisely because it admits of no 'solution' – promiscuity, repression, or the couple all being equally intolerable. Only a makeup of the Gethenian type, with its limitation of desire to a few days of the monthly cycle, could possibly curb the problem. Such a makeup suggests that sexual desire is something that can be completely removed from other human activities, allowing us to see in some more fundamental, unmixed fashion. (*AF*, 274)

The other social 'problem' Le Guin addresses is the problem of communication itself, but this time rather than conjure up an alien physiology she conceives of a machine, 'the ansible', whose unique property is to be able to communicate in real time across the galaxy irrespective of distance. On the one hand, this machine can be seen as answering a formal demand of the novel itself: if Ai has to timejump to get to the Gethen home-planet of Winter, with the result that all the family and friends he leaves behind will grow old and die in the few hours he spends on the spaceship, then his messages home, if they were to follow a similar pattern, would get back to Earth long after he himself had grown old and died, and more to the point, long after whatever he had reported on had passed into ancient history. But on the other hand, the machine is clearly intended to cut across such a 'wait and see' approach to communication, especially in its geopolitical context, a fact confirmed by its reappearance in Le Guin's more overtly political novels, her 1972 anti-Vietnam War work *The Word for World is Forest* and the slightly later *The Dispossessed* (1974). It might be seen, then, as a machine that cuts across the 'time' of uneven development, the present fact of global economics in other words, in which some nations are said to be 'developing' and others 'developed', or to put it more bluntly, some nations are stuck in the past while others are rocketing into the future. It is the persistence of such subliminal diachronic conceptions of the difference between the First and Third Worlds that holds at bay the more telling synchronic view which would hold that the Third World is as developed as it can be given the practices of the First World. So long as we continue to fantasize that the Third World is either well on the road to becoming like us, or somehow stubbornly resisting that eventuality, we fail to see the genuine differences. Moreover, by seeing the Third World as 'stuck in the past' we can blame their various problems, especially conflicts, on 'ancient' rivalries and other such pre-modern legacies the First World has supposedly outgrown.

Both of these examples testify to the one absolute of the entire genre of utopia, which is something Jameson calls 'disruption': the test of the utopian text, idea or impulse is whether or not its implementation 'disrupts' the present course of world history, forcing not merely some paradigmatic accommodation, but a wholesale syntagmatic transformation of the very syntax of society. Such ideas are difficult to come by; or rather, it is hard to think of examples of such ideas which do not ultimately have rather equivocal results (a fact that no doubt fuels the fear of utopia in the first place). Jameson's own such ambivalent example is the idea of universal employment. As he acknowledges, this idea runs counter to that other utopian ideal extolled by Marx's son-in-law, Paul Lafargue, namely the right to laziness, but the crucial point is that to realize universal employment in our present society would require enormous changes to not just the structure of our economy, but to the very ideology underpinning it, which as is well known regards unemployment as a necessary disciplining tool to keep wages low. As Clinton showed, though, it is perfectly possible to achieve universal employment if you simultaneously remove the restrictions on minimum wages and cut welfare benefits. So one has to modify the demand slightly and call for universal employment at a liveable wage, but just what that would be nobody knows and, economists say, is impossible to calculate anyway since the very situation of universal employment would almost certainly induce an increase in the rate of inflation. This in turn demands a further modification of the demand to include some kind of mechanism to keep check on inflation, thus ensuring that the gains of the demand are not then vaporized in a classic winner-loses scenario. By the same token, to even begin to imagine a world thus transformed is to indict our own present society for failing to live up to the promises it makes. Who could ever believe that this is the end of history as Fukuyama pronounced in 1989, as though to say things are as good as they can get? Utopia only comes into its own when we treat it as 'non-fiction', or in Deleuze's terms as a 'virtuality' (i.e., real without being actual) – only then do we see utopia is not some dreamt-up fantasy place where everything is miraculously 'better', but rather a cognitive procedure of determining what it is about our present world that must be changed to release us from its many known and unknown unfreedoms.

Conclusion

As the lines quoted in the epigraph above suggest, cognitive maps, here operating under the codename of ontologies of the present, demand of us archaeologies of the future, which is to say utopias.

Notes

1   This is not a reading of Deleuze and Guattari I happen to agree with, I should point out. In my view, it puts the cart before the horse because as I read them, Deleuze and Guattari argue that the tendency toward schizophrenia pre-exists capitalism and that capitalism merely exploits this potential to its fullest.

2   C. MacCabe, 'Preface' in F. Jameson *The Geopolitical Aesthetic: Cinema and Space in the World System* (London: BFI, 1992) p. xiv.

3   *SV*, 37.

4   'The relationship between class consciousness and figurability, in other words, demands something more basic than abstract knowledge, and implies a mode of experience that is more visceral and existential than the abstract certainties of economics and Marxian social science: the latter merely

continue to convince us of the informing presence, behind daily life, of the logic of capitalist production' (*SV*, 37–38).

5   See in particular the responses by Nancy Fraser and Cornel West (*CM*, 358–60).

6   L. Hutcheon, *The Politics of Postmodernism* (London: Routledge, 1989) p. 65. We might refuse this reading in another way as well: so-called magical realism, as practised by Rushdie, Grass and Márquez, is more totalizing than other kinds of realism, indeed other kinds of fiction, because it finds the means of giving figuration to the nonhistorical time (a) of collective memory; and (b) of the collective imaginary. One may also see it, as Franco Moretti does, as an absolution for colonialism granted by the victim, and in that sense an extremely reactionary form indeed. F. Moretti, *Modern Epic: The World System from Goethe to García Márquez* (trans. Q. Hoare; London: Verso, 1996) p. 250.

7   E. Hobsbawm, *The Age of Empire: 1875–1914* (London: Weidenfeld and Nicolson, 1987) p. 60.

8   It is worth noting here that while Jameson's (*U*, 133) first essay on Joyce does make mention of Kevin Lynch, the originator of the concept of 'cognitive mapping', and uses his ideas to describe Dublin, it does not give it the concept form it has now.

9   The keenest expression of this in the USA is to be found in the genre fiction of the period, particularly the western, whose primary invention 'the cowboy' is at once instrument and symptom of imperialist expansion. In Australia it was registered in the expressive realism of novels like Henry Handel Richardson's *The Fortunes of Richard Mahoney*, which maps the booms and busts of primary industries (gold mining and sheep farming in particular) against the feeling of existential ennui which the persistence of European manners and sensibilities induces in settlers.

Live Jameson

Ian Buchanan (IB): I'd like to start by asking you to describe your 'intellectual formation'.

Fredric Jameson (FJ): I'm a person of the 1950s rather than the 1960s (and whenever I say 'mine' or 'ours' of course I mean the United States as opposed to Europe, even though my formation is Eurocentric). My main affinities are really with France and Germany, but I have to register an early engagement with the Third World and particularly with Mexico in the 1950s, and also with the immense Islamic world that begins in North Africa and extends all the way to Indonesia. I travelled extensively in North Africa and of course North Africa is also very much a part of the French situation. I actually spent my first few weeks in Algeria – I imagine it must have been a month or two before the beginning of the Algerian revolution – when it was still very much a department of France, and a French colony, and so that figures in my background in ways that only maybe become evident later on in the 1960s. You have to remember that the most exciting and radical political event for white college students like myself in the 1950s was the whole business of McCarthyism and the Army/McCarthy hearings, I can't claim to have been much more radicalized than that when I went to Europe.

The crucial intellectual fact about the United States then and now is the utter absence of anything like what we would come to call western Marxism later on; my own contribution was (in books like *Marxism and Form*) to make that tradition known. I don't want to give myself any particular accolades, but I think I was probably the first to write on Adorno, on Bloch, maybe even Benjamin, and on Sartre's critique. That's a service that I'm still rather proud of. As for the actual task of Marxism in those days, you have to remember that this is long before anything called cultural studies, our essential focus was on literary criticism, and therefore it was as a way of devising new kinds of literary criticism that I conceived my first work: not merely introducing something that might generally or loosely be called Marxist literary criticism, the sociology of literature and so forth. We always wanted to distinguish this new 'method' very sharply from the old sociology of literature and culture and the latter very decisively from what Marxism did, but also to promote a specific twist and innovation in traditional Marxist criticism. Few of us who were working in this new area had any deep intellectual affinities with the older Soviet traditions and we understood the latter, as I guess everybody else did, as simply a matter of classifying works ideologically, and deciding whether they were progressive or conservative and so forth.

I think that the way I and others began to re-conceive this task was not simply to find out the ideological affinities of this or that writer, but in particular to see how the works of conservative or reactionary writers held features that one could consider progressive. So that evolved into an analysis of literary texts rather different from the older Marxist approaches. Then, later on, when 'theory' began (i.e., French theory, structuralism, post-structuralism, etc.), this kind of approach widened because it was necessary not only to take into account theoretical developments in Marxism but also to see how other theories that seemed either tangential to Marxism – or completely unrelated to it –, how those could be in a way appropriated for a new Marxist theorization. So in all of these ways I think the question was not to simply operate some political classifying system or class-affiliation analysis but to look for usable elements in both apolitical and anti-political literatures and in other philosophical traditions.

IB: In a number of interviews you have said that there were at least three people that you counted as being important teachers, Barthes, Benjamin and Sartre. And to follow up the previous question regarding your intellectual formation, could you give perhaps some kind of an account of how these three figures connect for you and how they actually contributed to your intellectual formation?

FJ: Well, I would say Adorno probably more than Benjamin, because Benjamin was still a figure that we knew only from various incidental pieces and not the work as a whole, something of course still coming into view and still very problematic as a coherent totality. But my first experience, even in college, I guess – maybe even before that – of the shock of recognition was with Sartre's work. There was in Sartre the possibility (that many people in that generation [also in France] felt) that suddenly you had a mode of analysis, of theorizing, of philosophizing, which could really philosophize about everything from daily life and existential experience all the way to politics and history. Freud was also always important to me: that was a great discovery and it intensified the feeling that everyday life itself was philosophical and that one could grasp it immanently. So, for me, my early work really comes out of Sartre, because the most important side of Barthes for me was *Writing Degree Zero*, *Mythologies*, the early works, and for me those were essentially prolongations of the Sartrean problematic.

Adorno was something else and I think I probably am not alone in having discovered Adorno not directly but through Thomas Mann's *Dr Faustus*, of which we obscurely learned that it was based on some unpublished musical manuscript which turned out to be *Philosophy of Modern Music*.

I began to discover Adorno's then-published texts when I studied in Germany (there weren't any translations at that point, I think). Through those texts, and only gradually, I came to realize that there was an alternative system of thinking in the German tradition which was more overtly dialectical, while the French tradition was overtly political. In the German tradition, on the other hand, negative dialectics was political in a situation in which they considered that politics had become impossible, so there one really had two possible alternatives: if political practice is still possible, you have the Sartrean model, and if there's a block or a stalemate, then in a way you have a very powerful countermodel in the German idea of keeping negative and critical thought alive. As it turns out, both of these had an influence on the American sixties, but given the presence of Marcuse, I suppose that it was the German tradition that much more openly influenced the American New Left and SDS.

IB: We tend to take the existence of theory for granted these days. What's difficult for someone from my generation to imagine is the sense of newness and necessity it must have had when it was first taken up. So I would like to ask you to paint a picture of what Anglo-American criticism was like such that theory seemed like a radical option.

FJ: Well American criticism at that point was really the New Criticism, with some embellishments and deviations. I think Frye was not so influential in those days, but then we already had myth criticism and various other kinds of things. But they were all exclusively literary and I think you have to understand that in English departments – in my own college, Haverford College, for example – literature went up really only to Browning, and indeed Browning was a little too hard, so in effect they really only went up to Tennyson. Whereas I was formed in French and in French departments where people were reading the most advanced contemporary texts all the time and where, very importantly, politics were not subject to Anglo-American censorship, so that a proper French department even in the 1950s understood that the leftwing writers were also great French writers, writers in a specifically French anti-bourgeois tradition from Balzac on down. So that's an important local piece of the puzzle. The diffusion of theory in the United States, was in that regard quite different from other countries: it really took place first and foremost through French departments, and our departmental structure in the American system was such that we really could have an effect well beyond the immediate French curriculum. Whereas I understand that in England, French teachers were really very severely limited to French literature as such and that the diffusion of theory came on the contrary through the public sphere via journals like *New Left Review*. So it was not so much any resistance to literature that was basic here, but only the idea that literature and culture was something a little more significant than mere belles-lettres.

There, too, my background was a little bit different: instead of the New Criticism, I was really formed in what I guess you could very largely call philology, in both French and German; style studies, as it was called then, the work of people like Auerbach for example, who was my teacher at Yale, where the relationship of the individual text and the style and the words and so forth, to movements and historical contexts was a great deal closer and more intimate than the purely aesthetic appreciations of most English departments. So that also paved the way for an interest in theory. But it was really the opening up of much larger questions about the relationship of something called language and textuality to something called the social, the opening up in Sartre by way of the structural anthropology of Lévi-Strauss and myth criticism – Lévi-Strauss's myth criticism, I mean – and the whole notion of how narrative functions in the world of the social and the ideological fully as much as in literature; also important was the Barthesian notion of ideology, developed in *Mythologies*. It was all of those things that made us understand that in literature, we had a set of new experimental situations that the social sciences didn't yet perceive, and I suppose one has to say that this was a kind of imperialism of the newer theoretical humanities with respect not only to the study of literatures in the other languages, but also with respect to the social sciences. This was the first really pioneering mission that we may have derived through the synthesis in French structuralism of linguistics and anthropology and Marxism. It was really a whole new revolution in method that was being pioneered in the humanities and gradually over a long period of time having its ultimate impact on the other disciplines.

IB: What I've always found to be particularly distinctive about your work is the way in which style always connects to politics, the way in which close attention to the issue of how the text is formed becomes the crucial means of understanding its ideological reference. I also want to pick up on an earlier point: you said that part of what you wanted to do was to look for the progressive elements within the reactionary. Perhaps you could link these two points together and say something about your way of reading texts.

FJ: Well, let's take the matter of style first because it's crucial and can explain some of the later turns that you are interested in, namely the emergence of theories of postmodernism. As I said, I was formed in the style-studies tradition coming out of Spitzer and Auerbach and also in a modern way very much exemplified by some of the great literary essays of Sartre himself on Faulkner, in *Situations*, volume 1 (I don't know how it's configured in the English translations). But it was under the impact of Barthes's reading of literary history in *Writing Degree Zero* that I began to come to the idea that style was a specifically modern or modernist phenomena. That is to say, I began to conceive the idea that the invention of a personal style was linked up to a whole construction of the individual subject in modernism, and that therefore stylistic variations had within them not only a whole worldview as this method presupposed, but also offered specific clues to the dubious and indeed suspect political and oppositional leanings of writers like Wyndham Lewis. So the postmodern thread in all this is the apprehension – and I think Barthes sensed this very early in his notion of white writing, but perhaps prematurely – that style itself was coming to an end and that modernism itself ends with the exhaustion of the possibilities of producing a whole new style. Something else, something new, then presumably begins which is rather difficult to describe. Nobody thinks that people like David Foster Wallace are styleless, but rather that the production of the individual or personal style – maybe even what you find in Pynchon – is no longer of the same order as modernist style and in that sense the transformation in the very possibility of producing style gets linked to the great post-structural theoretical problematic of the so-called 'death of the subject', the end of centred subjectivity. So the matter of style and its possibilities is very much at stake in the later philosophical developments.

So that's one way in which my earlier more literary work really does lead via this social and systemic mutation into theories of postmodernity. Now, on the other matter of progressive or reactionary elements I suppose that we were all a little embarrassed by such inherited terms and so what occurred to me was a rather different term, namely that of the utopian, because it gradually seemed to me – as one looks at, I don't say necessarily only fascist writers, but at the whole of what Spinoza would call the 'sad passions' of right-wing literature and culture – that nonetheless even those ideologies insofar as they draw on a whole set of collective desires, are somehow also collective and thus harbour deep within themselves a kind of utopian impulse. So, little by little, that notion and that term came to suggest a new revision of the older Marxist methodological agenda.

Now, for example, we know that both Flaubert and Baudelaire had very sympathetic and indeed utopian commitments to the Revolution of 1848. It is not in merely looking for interesting biographical facts of that kind that one sorts out the progressive and the reactionary, but in the realization that even within achieved reactionary or, let's say, even apolitical and liberal works, if they are of sufficient energy, one ought to be able to find the informing drive of what I think it's best to call, the utopian impulse. This conviction then secures a whole different agenda for cultural study, that is to say, identifying that impulse of collectivity and reflecting on the ways in which it can be made available, not only in culture but in social and political action. That's a rather different way of configuring the political commitment to literary and cultural studies than the old method of classification in terms of right and left wing.

IB: That then prompts a question about method. Your work offers the possibility of reading a text in a multiply-layered way. Could you perhaps explain a bit further how the idea of reading texts in layers enables you to read dialectically.

FJ: The text is a kind of 'libidinal apparatus', which can be invested by a number of forces and meanings. Certainly, all texts are open to the identification with gender ideologies, but by the same token they're also open to investment by a whole range of other levels of desire and of what one could call ideological orientation, and those would include race and class, they would include the national situation itself and a host of other more specific determinations. The analysis of the text is never limited by any one of those, although a powerful analysis of the text on any one of those thematic registers always tends to tell us something striking and important. Yet the text remains this porous and receptive object that soaks up all such complicated and coexistent levels of fantasy or desire. Of course one never reaches a point in which one understands everything and in which one has a total understanding of the text because every new readership brings some new ones, but as a methodological precept it seems to me it's very important to keep alive this notion of the openness of the multiplicity of these determinations. Now, I don't happen to like the word 'open' very much, because this has been drummed into us ideologically as 'open' versus 'closed' societies and 'open' versus 'closed' philosophical systems – a truly tendentious and ideological Cold War concept, which has as its ideological opposite number the idea that, well, if such determinations are insufficient then one should speak in more general terms about the indeterminacy of the text. I would rather talk about the multiple determinations of the text thus leaving open the possibility for still more of those, rather than to impose some ideological vision of either opposition – open versus closed or that between indeterminacy or the postmodern aleatory and this or that old-fashioned closure. It seems to me the question isn't there, but that it's on this possibility of multiple investments in a text that one should focus.

IB: What I'm wondering now is how analysis begins in the postmodern? If personal or individual style has vanished with the end of modernism, if there is no distinctiveness left to focus on to connect to the ideological in a straightforward way, it seems to me that would then present a very new and obviously very difficult situation for the analysis of text.

FJ: Well, it is also a question about the changeover in my own work from the analysis of specific texts to the analysis of, let's say, postmodern formations, and it is a very difficult one. One has to come at it in indirect or mediated ways. One has to say first of all that in that sense the older text, the older textual object, whether literary or artistic, cognitive or rhetorical, has been in a very real sense volatilized. A lot of people have talked about this disappearance of the work of art or the art object, the way in which the great individual aesthetic object of the easel painting has been refracted into clusters like installation art or displaced by the concept; the way in which even the older notion of the literary work or masterpiece has been volatilized into a whole host of cultural or mass cultural movements. At that point clearly some new form of analysis is necessary and it seemed to me that that kind of analysis had to come from, let's say, the patterning system of postmodernity itself, the way in which all of these objects no longer function as the expression of an individual subjectivity, but participate in some larger movement of the cultural production of late capitalism or postmodernity. That clearly demands a different kind of analysis from the old *explication de texte*.

One wants to say that the danger here would lie in taking all these new aesthetic objects as mere examples of some larger cultural tendency. On the other hand, the problem with that objection is that they aren't really individual objects anymore, they are to use the language of post-structuralism, forms of textuality in the very stream of postmodern culture, and they must therefore necessarily be grasped in another way. It thus becomes a question of the role of culture itself or of specific forms of culture, like literature, in a situation in which, as I've said many times, culture itself has been enormously expanded, in which the entire economic system has in a way itself become cultural and in which we don't have the reassurances of this individual object of study any longer to guide our specific work or our specific readings. But surely some kind of rigour can be imagined in this new situation as well; it doesn't simply open things up to some vague and general cultural criticism, at least I hope that that wouldn't be the case. I've always, in my own work, been concerned to discredit the whole ambition of what I call 'culture critique' in this vague sociological and mass-cultural sense. It seems to me that it's slogans like 'other directedness', the 'culture of narcissism', and even the Frankfurt School notions of the 'authoritarian personality', the work of Eric Fromm that was associated with the Frankfurt School, indeed, Foucauldian 'capillary power', are really pop-psychological substitutes for genuine political and social and economic analysis of the present.

IB: You are on record as saying we need the problematic of Marxism more than ever in confronting late capitalism today, but we have to invent new solutions. This prompts two questions: (i) What is the Marxist problematic today, what form does it take? (ii) What are some of the new solutions that are available or that can be imagined?

FJ: Well, as for the new solutions, I don't know; I mean that if we could imagine them we'd have them already, so that may be more difficult to foresee. But even without the 'new solutions' the strengths of the Marxist problematic are twofold: one is the conception of the commodity which is a structural rather than a moral or an ethical one, and therefore one which leads us into a politics about consumerism and commodification which doesn't involve an ethical impulse easily degenerating into Puritanism and other fanaticisms; the other is the Marxian idea of the economic system which is powerful. My impression as an outsider is that all other types of economics as they're practised today are purely pragmatic and empirical and offer recipes and remedies for this or that specific aspect of production or distribution, or specific recommendations for investment, or for the restructuring of finance; whereas the strength of Marxian economics is that it is really the only approach that considers the system as a whole. Both these strengths of Marxism, however, reflect a perspective that was maybe not so binding in previous moments and previous forms of Marxist politics. Culture was the moment of truth of so-called western Marxism: to have insisted on the cultural dimension of capitalism. And we are now, with globalization and postmodernity, in a moment in which these cultural issues become absolutely central. One might also speak as Lefebvre does in some of his last books about the spatialization of politics: Lefebvre calls indeed for a new kind of spatial dialectic. Perhaps that is the direction in which some new conception of a Marxist politics might move, but I'm sure there are many other possible formulations that we're not even aware of yet.

IB: In several places you have said that theory has replaced philosophy, implying that philosophy has somehow vanished. Could you explain a little more what you mean by saying philosophy is vanishing?

FJ: One can register after the very effervescent period of the 1970s and 1980s, a palpable reversion of philosophy to its traditional sub-fields and its various subdivisions such as ethics, political philosophy and metaphysics and so forth and I do think that is an unfortunate symptom of a decline in philosophical speculation. After all, in the history of philosophy since Hegel (if you take Nietzsche as the kick-off point of newer philosophy) there's always been a critique of philosophy as such, a critique of the philosophical system. I don't doubt that there will continue to be brilliant philosophers as we've had them in the past, but I suspect that the force of their thought will come from resisting those traditional domains and launching out in all kinds of new things rather than in the boring and perpetual defence of the status of philosophy itself. One can certainly observe within the work of most philosophers one crucial concern which is to re-theorize philosophy and to justify the practice that they're involved in, and this even when one reaches such truly original and idiosyncratic thinkers as Deleuze and Derrida. Yet in a way, theory or what I would rather call 'theoretical discourse' or 'theoretical writing' is at least freed from that kind of necessity of self-defence. It is something that in philosophy makes the now-classic critical attack of Pierre Bourdieu very plausible indeed, for whom all of these disciplines end up simply being self-justifications and ingenious self-serving schemes for the re-establishment and continuation of the discipline itself. So one way of coming at the distinctiveness of theoretical writing as such lies in its formal liberation from that seeming instinct for self-preservation of the discipline that one continues to find in traditional philosophy. I would regard people like Deleuze and Derrida, whom I've mentioned, as being philosophers who pushed at the limits of philosophy to the point where they do theory and are theorists, in spite of their philosophical self-definitions rather than because of those things. But I read philosophy passionately myself and the philosophical tradition is absolutely a part of everything one does in theory today and so I would wish this criticism to be taken structurally rather than in any hostile or ideological sense.

IB: This is perhaps the moment then to ask you about myth criticism because very interestingly you have suggested that there may be a proper use of myth criticism (in spite of your criticisms of it), but only if it is affirmed that our situation today is different from that of primitive society. Do you still think myth criticism has a place or can be reinvented in a way that would be useful today?

FJ: This is a very tricky question. Benjamin asked himself this question in his *Arcades Project* and was attentive to the critiques of the Frankfurt School who were maybe more alert than he was at that point to the affinities of myth criticism with Jungianism and even a kind of fascist affirmation in it of the archaic impulses that fascism and nazism tried to resurrect. Clearly a myth criticism which takes that route is unacceptable. I would myself also want to say that sociobiology is a kind of positivist version of this same effort in that it attempts to link very complex modern societies back to the simplest of biological urges and thereby to simplify social reality in a way which is also mythic, although it certainly doesn't look very much like Jungianism. The Marxist perspective on this is of course that these very archaic societies were also societies without power and without money: whether one would call all of them forms of primitive communism is much more complicated since of course some of them had caste systems and an aristocracy and all the rest of it. But it seems to me that the greatness of Lévi-Strauss was to reopen a powerful path back to the social realities of those archaic societies and to all kinds of social relationships which we have lost in the modern industrial capitalist world. It is not so much a matter of recreating those things as it is a tapping of a properly utopian energy that's present in those older societies and that one can find in primitive myths. The point is not to re-mythologize our present, but to use this moment of the distant human past (as with other modes of production in the past) as a way of understanding what we've lost historically and as a charge of utopian energy on which we can draw. So, while on the one hand I'm certainly very interested in what myths understood in that sense have to offer us, on the other I'm very apprehensive about all of the misconceptions that the very notion of myth as a positive value can bring into being and those are in my opinion for the most part ideological and deserve to be examined with the greatest of suspicion.

IB: In a number of places you've said that today we suffer from an inability to imagine the future. Do you think this is still the case? If so, do you see any possible remedies?

FJ: I think it's very difficult for people today to imagine the future as anything but the prolongation of what already exists – as Benjamin says, the catastrophe is not something awaiting us, but is simply the fact that all this goes on, continues to go on, exactly as it does. It's obviously impossible for human beings to exist without a sense of the future (that's the burden of, if you like, Sartrean existentialism or of any other ambitious and demanding phenomenology of human consciousness). But many things interfere with a productive use of those impulses towards the future, and one needs to find ways to unblock those impulses.

Even in the realm of technology, if one goes back to the beginning of the industrial period in the late nineteenth century, there were all kinds of wonder-working visions of science-fictional futures. It seems to me that those are much less operative today; we essentially think that there'll be tinkerings – ever smaller kinds of computer chips and so forth – but that essentially all this will remain the same. The merit of people like Paul Virilio and Manuel DeLanda is that they too have attempted to reinvent and to reopen a notion of future technological change which restores at least some forms of future development and future consciousness in that particular area, although I tend to feel that their efforts, like Baudrillard's, are essentially of a visionary and poetic type. My own method, which has seemed to many people to be frustrating and pessimistic, is to concentrate on ways in which we cannot imagine the future. It has seemed to me that something would be achieved if we began to realize how firmly we are locked into a present without a future and to get a sense of all the things that limit our imagination of the future. I suppose this is a Brechtian device in the sense that Brecht always wanted us to understand that the things that we consider to be natural and eternal are really only historical and constructed and thereby can be changed. Even though the idea of nature has vanished from postmodernity, there's much that we still continue to think of in what used to be natural terms as eternal features of this situation we're in: so that we can easily imagine, as I've said in *The Seeds of Time*, the destruction of the world through whatever catastrophe, but have much more difficulty imagining the end of capitalism and its replacement by something else. My method in this area and in the utopian area generally has been a negative one, that is, it's to examine the blockages on the future and on the utopian impulse rather than to propose positive new utopian visions of the type the nineteenth century in its crucial utopian moments projected so brilliantly, from Fourier to Morris.

IB: In *Marxism and Form* you say a successful application of the dialectic should produce a shock, a glimpse of the real, so asking what is probably a stupid question, how would you instruct students to do it, how would you begin to explain how one should go about constructing the dialectic, applying it, and eventually producing that shock? Because ultimately, and this is something else you say, your role as an intellectual is to teach and to instruct, so perhaps you can offer some advice on how to do this.

FJ: Well, I guess I'm tempted to begin an answer to that question by repeating the Sartrean, Heideggerian, maybe even Lacanian idea that we're never in the truth, we're always in error, *méconnaissance*, various ideology, illusions of all kinds and that the truth is not a place that we can remain in, even though every so often we can have fitful glimpses of that truth and try to hold on to a moment of authenticity that's constantly slipping away, imperilled on all sides, and necessarily condemned to disappear into ideology and reification. Human beings are always inauthentic but are occasionally capable of some moment of authenticity. I wanted to insist on the way in which a genuine dialectical thought really has that shock of repositioning ourselves for a brief moment in the truth or in authenticity, but only for a fitful moment. I'm not sure that this can be taught except by example – I don't mean by my personal example, but by examples of moments in which all of a sudden we grasp this larger movement of the dialectic. If one is thinking about contemporary history, for example, the recent past is always the most obscure to all of us and the great analyses of present history are those which suddenly make clear and vivid the immediate links between a current situation and all kinds of things in that immediate past that we'd forgotten or whose relationship to the present we had never really understood before. There are many ways in which one gets these flashes of dialectical insight and the pedagogical method would lie in holding on to a few of those and showing them in operation in order for us to understand what that momentary revelation consists in and then to be more alert to it and open to it in the future. But I really don't think there is a method to be taught, except on the most banal levels, for thinking dialectically. Or else that's the task of the reading of previous thinkers. In Hegel, Marx, as well as in lots of other seemingly non-dialectical writers, we do experience the dialectic at work and there, too, we can retroactively learn some of those lessons. But, it isn't something one can apply then in a cut-and-dried way and this is the problem with all concepts of method.

IB: Thank you.

Bibliography

Works by Jameson

Archaeologies of the Future: The Desire Called Utopia and Other Science Fictions (London: Verso, 2005).

'Symptoms of Theory or Symptoms for Theory?', *Critical Inquiry* 30:2 (2004) pp. 403–408.

'On Representing Globalisation' (unpublished paper presented at 'Globalisation and Indigenous Cultures' conference, Zhengzhow University, China, 2004) pp. 1–27.

'*Dekalog* as *Decameron*', in D. Kellner and S. Homer (eds) *Fredric Jameson: A Critical Reader* (London: Palgrave, 2004) pp. 210–22.

'Marc Angenot, Literary History, and the Study of Culture in the Nineteenth Century', *The Yale Journal of Criticism* 17:2 (2004) pp. 233–53.

'Future City', *New Left Review* 2 21 (2003) pp. 65–79.

'The End of Temporality', *Critical Inquiry* 29 (2003) pp. 695–718.

A Singular Modernity: Essay on the Ontology of the Present (London: Verso, 2002).

'From Metaphor to Allegory', in C. Davidson (ed.), *Anything* (Cambridge, Mass.: The MIT Press, 2001) pp. 25–36.

'Globalisation and Political Strategy', *New Left Review* 2 4 (2000) pp. 49–68.

The Cultural Turn: Selected Writings on the Postmodern, 1983–1998 (London: Verso, 1998).

'Notes on Globalisation as a Philosophical Issue', in F. Jameson and M. Miyoshi (eds), *The Cultures of Globalisation* (Durham: Duke University Press, 1998) pp. 54–77.

'Marxism and the Historicity of Theory: An Interview with Fredric Jameson', *New Literary History* 29:3 (1998) pp. 354–83.

Brecht and Method (London: Verso, 1998).

'Persistencies of the Dialectic: Three Sites', *Science and Society*, 62:3 (1998) pp. 358–72.

'Interview with Fredric Jameson', in E. Corredor (ed.), *Lukács After Communism: Interviews with Contemporary Intellectuals* (London: Duke University Press, 1997).

'Marx's Purloined Letter', *New Left Review* 209.4 (1995) pp. 86–120

The Seeds of Time (New York: Columbia University Press, 1994).

'Americans Abroad: Exogamy and Letters in Late Capitalism', in S. Bell *et al.* (eds) *Critical Theory, Cultural Politics, and Latin American Narratives* (Notre Dame and London: University of Notre Dame Press, 1993) pp. 35–60.

'On Cultural Studies', *Social Text* 34 (1993) pp. 17–52.

Signatures of the Visible (London: Routledge, 1992).

The Geopolitical Aesthetic: Cinema and Space in the World System (London: BFI Publishing, 1992).

Postmodernism, or, the Cultural Logic of Late Capitalism (Durham: Duke University Press, 1991).

Late Marxism: Adorno, or, The Persistence of the Dialectic (London: Verso, 1990).

'Regarding Postmodernism: A Conversation with Fredric Jameson', in D. Kellner (ed.), *Postmodernism, Jameson, Critique* (Washington, DC: Maisonneuve Press, 1989) pp. 43–74.

The Ideologies of Theory: Essays 1971–1986. Volume 1: *Situations of Theory* (Minneapolis: University of Minnesota Press, 1988).

The Ideologies of Theory: Essays 1971–1986. Volume 2: *Syntax of History* (Minneapolis: University of Minnesota Press, 1988).

'Modernism and Imperialism', *Nationalism, Colonialism and Literature (Field Day Pamphlet 14)* (Derry: Field Day Theatre Company, 1988).

'Cognitive Mapping', in C. Nelson and L. Grossberg (eds), *Marxism and the Interpretation of Culture* (London: MacMillan, 1988) pp. 347–60.

'Foreword', in Algirdas Julien Greimas *On Meaning: Selected Writings in Semiotics Theory* (trans. Paul J. Perron and Frank H. Collins; Minneapolis: University of Minnesota Press, 1987).

'Third-World Literature in the Era of Multinational Capitalism', *Social Text* 15 (1986) pp. 65–88.

Sartre: The Origins of a Style (New York: Columbia University Press, 1984 [1961]).

'Flaubert's Libidinal Historicism: *Trois Contes*', in N. Schor and H. Majewski (eds) *Flaubert and Postmodernism* (Lincoln and London: University of Nebraska Press, 1984) pp. 76–83.

'Wallace Stevens', *New Orleans Review* 11:1 (1984) pp. 10–19.

'Rimbaud and the Spatial Text', in T. Wong and M.A. Abbas (eds), *Rewriting Literary History* (Hong Kong: Hong Kong University Press, 1984) pp. 66–93.

'Foreword', in Jean-François Lyotard, *The Postmodern Condition: A Report on Knowledge* (trans. G. Bennington and B. Massumi; Minneapolis: University of Minnesota Press, 1984) pp. vii–xxi.

'"Ulysses" in History', in W.J. McCormack and A. Stead (eds), *James Joyce and Modern Literature* (London: Routledge and Kegan Paul, 1982) pp. 126–41.

The Political Unconscious: Narrative as a Socially Symbolic Act (London: Routledge, 1981).

Fables of Aggression: Wyndham Lewis, the Modernist as Fascist (Berkeley: University of California Press, 1979).

'Towards a Libidinal Economy of Three Modern Painters', *Social Text* 1:1 (1979) pp. 189–99.

'History and the Death Wish: *Zardoz* as Open Form', *Jump Cut* 3 (1974) 5–8.

The Prison-House of Language: A Critical Account of Structuralism and Russian Formalism (Princeton: Princeton University Press, 1972).

'The Great American Hunter: Ideological Content in the Novel', *College English* 34 (1972) pp. 180–97.

Marxism and Form: Twentieth-Century Dialectical Theories of Literature (Princeton: Princeton University Press, 1971).

Works by other writers

Agamben, G., *Means without End: Notes on Politics* (trans. V. Binetti and C. Casarino; Minneapolis: University of Minnesota Press, 2000).

Anderson, B., *Imagined Communities: Reflections on the Origins and Spread of Nationalism* (London: Verso, 1983).

Anderson, P., *The Origins of Postmodernity* (London: Verso, 1998).

—— *A Zone of Engagement* (London: Verso, 1992).

Barthes, R., *The Pleasure of the Text* (trans. R. Miller; New York: Hill and Wang, 1975).

Belsey, C., *Critical Practice* (London: Routledge, 2000).

Benjamin, W., *One-Way Street* (trans. E. Jephcott and K. Shorter; London: Verso, 1979).

—— *Charles Baudelaire: A Lyric Poet in the Era of High Capitalism* (trans. H. Zohn; London: Verso, 1973).

Biskind, P., *Easy Riders, Raging Bulls: How the Sex 'n' Drugs 'n' Rock 'n' Roll Generation Saved Hollywood* (London: Bloomsbury, 1999).

Bourdieu, P., *The Field of Cultural Production: Essays on Art and Literature* (Cambridge: Polity Press, 1993).

Brown, B., 'The Dark Wood of Postmodernity (Space, Faith, Allegory), *PMLA*, 120:3 (2005) pp. 734–50.

Buchanan, I., 'The Counter-Revolution in the Revolution', *Arena Journal* 25–26 (2006) pp. 83–98.

—— 'National Allegory Today – A Return to Jameson', in C. Irr and I. Buchanan (eds), *On Jameson: From Postmodernism to Globalisation* (New York: SUNY Press, 2006) pp. 173–88.

—— 'Space in the Age of Non-Place', in I. Buchanan and G. Lambert (eds) *Deleuze and Space* (Edinburgh: Edinburgh University Press, 2005) pp. 16–35.

—— 'Inevitable Fusion? King Kong and the Libeskind Spire', *Antithesis* 14 (2004) pp. 170–74.

—— 'Reading Jameson Dogmatically', *Historical Materialism* 10:3 (2002) pp. 223–43.

—— *Deleuzism: A Metacommentary* (Edinburgh: Edinburgh University Press, 2000).

Butler, R., *Slavoj Žižek: Live Theory* (New York and London: Continuum, 2005).

Callinicos, A., *Against Postmodernism: A Marxist Critique* (Cambridge: Polity Press, 1989).

Chakrabarty, D., *Provincialising Europe: Postcolonial Thought and Historical Difference* (Princeton: Princeton University Press, 2000).

Clark, T.J., *Farewell to an Idea: Episodes from a History of Modernism* (New Haven: Yale University Press, 1999).

Davis, M., 'Planet of Slums: Urban Involution and the Informal Proletariat', *New Left Review 2* 26 (2004) pp. 5–34.

——— 'Urban Renaissance and the Spirit of Postmodernism', *New Left Review* 151 (1985) 106–13.

Davis, M., *et al. Under the Perfect Sun: The San Diego Tourists Never See* (New York: The New Press, 2003).

Deleuze, G., *The Logic of Sense* (trans. M. Lester with C. Stivale; London: Athlone Press, 1990).

——— *Cinema 2: The Time-Image* (trans. H. Tomlinson and R. Galeta; Minneapolis: University of Minnesota Press, 1989).

Deleuze, G. and F. Guattari, *What is Philosophy?* (trans. H. Tomlinson and G. Burchell; London: Verso, 1994).

——— *A Thousand Plateaus* (trans. B. Massumi; Minneapolis: University of Minnesota Press, 1987).

Derrida, J., 'Marx & Sons', in M. Sprinker (ed.) *Ghostly Demarcations: A Symposium on Jacques Derrida's Spectres of Marx* (London: Verso, 1999) pp. 213–62.

During, S., 'Postmodernism or Post-Colonialism Today', *Textual Practice*, 1:1 (1987) pp. 32–67.

Eagleton, T., 'Making a Break', *London Review of Books* 28:5 (2006) pp. 25–6.

——— *Walter Benjamin, or Towards a Revolutionary Criticism* (London: Verso, 1981).

Foster, H., *Design and Crime (And Other Diatribes)* (London: Verso, 2002).

Frye, N., *Anatomy of Criticism* (London: Penguin, 1957).

Gowan, P., *The Global Gamble: Washington's Faustian Bid for World Dominance* (London: Verso, 1999).

Greenblatt, S., 'Who Killed Christopher Marlowe', *The New York Review of Books* LIII: 6 (2006) pp. 42–46.

Gregory, D., *Geographical Imaginations* (Oxford: Blackwell, 1994).

Hardt, M. and A. Negri, *Multitude: War and Democracy in the Age of Empire* (London: Hamish Hamilton, 2004).

——— *Empire* (Cambridge, Mass.: Harvard University Press, 2000).

Harvey, D., *The Condition of Postmodernity: An Enquiry into the Origins of Cultural Change* (Cambridge: Blackwell, 1990).

Henwood, D., *After the New Economy* (New York: The New Press, 2003).

Hobsbawm, E., *The Age of Empire: 1875–1914* (London: Weidenfeld and Nicolson, 1987).

Hutcheon, L., *The Politics of Postmodernism* (London: Routledge, 1989).

——— *A Poetics of Postmodernism: History, Theory, Fiction* (London: Routledge, 1988).

Klein, N., *No Logo* (London: Flamingo, 2000).

Lévi-Strauss, C., *Tristes Tropiques* (trans. J. and D. Weightman; London: Penguin Books, 1992).
—— *The Savage Mind* (Chicago: Chicago University Press, 1966).
Lurie, A., 'The Passion of C.S. Lewis', *The New York Review of Books* LIII:2 (2006) pp. 10–13.
Lyotard, J.-L., *The Postmodern Condition: A Report on Knowledge* (trans. G. Bennington and B. Massumi; Minneapolis: University of Minnesota Press, 1984).
MacCabe, C., 'Preface', in F. Jameson, *The Geopolitical Aesthetic: Cinema and Space in the World System* (London: BFI, 1992).
Massumi, B., *Parables for the Virtual: Movement, Affect, Sensation* (Durham, NC: Duke University Press, 2002).
Moretti, F., *Modern Epic: The World System from Goethe to García Márquez* (trans. Q. Hoare; London: Verso, 1996).
Parenti, C., *Lockdown America: Police and Prisons in the Age of Crisis* (London: Verso, 1999).
Said, E., *Out of Place: A Memoir* (London: Granta, 1999)
Sontag, S., *Against Interpretation* (London: Vintage, 2001).
Szeman, I., *Zones of Instability: Literature, Postcolonialism, and the Nation* (Baltimore: The Johns Hopkins University Press, 2003).
Venturi, R., D. Scott Brown and S. Izenour, *Learning from Las Vegas: The Forgotten Symbolism of Architectural Form* (Cambridge, Mass.: The MIT Press, 1972).
West, C., 'Fredric Jameson's Marxist Hermeneutics', *Boundary 2* 11:1–2 (1982) pp. 177–200.
White, H., *The Content of the Form: Narrative Discourse and Historical Representation* (Baltimore: The Johns Hopkins University Press, 1987).
Willis, S., *Portents of the Real: A Primer for Post-9/11 America* (London: Verso, 2005).
Wollen, P., *Readings and Writings* (London: Verso, 1982).
Žižek, S., 'Between Two Deaths', *London Review of Books* 26 (2004) p. 11.
—— *Tarrying with the Negative: Kant, Hegel, and the Critique of Ideology* (Durham, NC: Duke University Press, 1993).
—— *The Sublime Object of Ideology* (London: Verso, 1990).

Index